Southern Landscape and Garden Design

Southern Landscape

Pacesetter Press
A Division of Gulf Publishing Company
Houston, London, Paris, Tokyo

and Garden Design

James Carroll Kell

Library of Congress Cataloging in Publication Data

Kell, James Carroll.
    Southern landscape and garden design.

    Includes index.
    1. Landscape gardening. 2. Landscape
architecture. 3. Landscape gardening—Southern
States. I. Title.
SB473.K47   712   80-473
ISBN 0-88415-811-X

Illustrations on pages
2, 7, 9, 10, 11, 12, 13, and 15
by the author

Illustration on page 20
by Steven Vermie

Other illustrations
by Terry J. Moore

Edited by
B. J. Lowe

Book Design by
Leigh Owen

Contents

Designing with Plants, 71

Landscape Planning and Design Kit, 82

Southern Landscape Plants, 100

Index, 111

of special interest...

for Kathleen, my patient sufferer
Scott, my trusty helper
and Princess and Buffy, my faithful companions

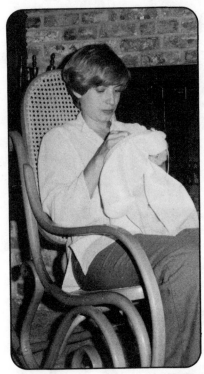

Patient Sufferer

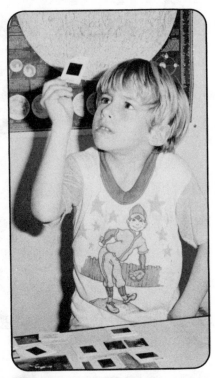

Helper

Faithful Companions

Preface

For me, as for most authors, the beginning is the end. Having written the book, I now have the opportunity to write *about* it.

My main goal has been to create a practical manual of home landscape design that you can use in planning and designing for yourself the landscape development of your home grounds. This is a How-To-Design-It, not a How-To-Build-It, book.

It begins with a step-by-step planning procedure to help you organize your efforts. Next, some background information in the form of basic principles and concepts of landscape design is presented, followed by a nuts-and-bolts presentation of the many design details involved in the home landscape from bottom to top.

Then, the various concepts involved in the design of each home landscape space, from the front yard all the way around the house, are explored. And finally, the subject of planting design, an integral part of the total landscape design process, is singled out for a closer look.

Throughout the book you'll find references to the "KIT" at the back. This is a compilation of supplementary information you'll find necessary as you work your way through each step of the design process.

One of the most significant things for the reader of any instructional book to realize is that none is complete. For years I have searched for the mythical "Complete Book Of Gardening." None exists, except in title; nor will there ever be one. Therefore, the seeker of wholeness must collect several "complete" books on a given subject.

Likewise, books discussing design theory and practice must ultimately subscribe to one basic approach which colors all aspects discussed. This is proper and acceptable—but incomplete.

The logical conclusion is that this book is incomplete—and I'll be the first to admit that it is. I therefore recommend that you search out other landscape design books to fill in any gaps which, for you, this book leaves unfilled.

James Carroll Kell
February 1980

ix

Pacesetter Press:
*A Tradition of Excellence
in Southern Gardening—*

Vegetable Growing for Southern Gardens
Southern Flower Gardening
Southern Lawns and Groundcovers
Shrubs and Vines for Southern Landscapes
Trees for Southern Landscapes
Herb Gardening in the South
Growing Fruits, Berries, & Nuts in the South
Tropical Gardening Along the Gulf Coast
Greenhouse Gardening in the South
Southern Gardener's Soil Handbook
Southern Landscape and Garden Design

*Other Quality Pacesetter Books
Southerners Will Enjoy—*

A Guide to Hunting in Texas
Camper's Guide to Texas Parks, Lakes, and Forests
Beachcomber's Guide to Gulf Coast Marine Life
Backroads of Texas
Hiking and Backpacking Trails of Texas

How to Plan Your Landscape

> **Planning:** An orderly process of analysis and synthesis leading to the accomplishment of an endeavor.

Planning is an important activity in everyone's life. Perhaps you plan your daily work schedule, or the evening meal, or the monthly budget. Even if your daily routine is somewhat disorganized, you surely plan for major events such as the purchase of a home or a change to a new job. Whether or not you're conscious of the process, you are analyzing the situation (taking stock, sizing up the problems) to determine all the facts before putting them together (synthesis) into a plan of action. It may take seconds, hours, or days, but the process is the same for every planning endeavor, and that includes landscape planning.

The Big Picture

Why Plan?

Most of us have a tendency to concentrate too quickly on details; to see the trees instead of the forest; to collect a piece at a time with no thought to the nature of the final collection; or to practice curative instead of preventive medicine. The results of this approach can be readily seen in the front yard landscapes of many suburban homes. There you'll often find a horticultural collection of incompatible plants, poorly arranged, and in the wrong places. Just as bad, each yard looks much like the next, revealing that many homeowners took the shallow approach of copying what someone else had done rather than responding to the needs of their specific situations.

Why then should you plan the development of your home grounds? To make your yard prettier than your neighbor's or to make it different? No. The basic goal of landscape planning is to maximize the beauty and function of your entire site in a manner that will allow you the most enjoyment of life. This means complete planning of your total living environment—both inside the house and out in the yard—as a unit. Through landscape planning you can take all those great ideas you've seen in home and garden magazines or gleaned from your neighbor and translate them into a unified solution which reflects your lifestyle and at the same time responds to the constraints and advantages of your climate and site.

Many homeowners undertake one small landscape project after another in bite-size chunks they can afford. There's nothing wrong with this except that you usually have no clear idea how each project will relate to future ones. A better approach is to first prepare a master landscape development plan for the entire site as you would ultimately like it to be, and then accomplish the various portions of the plan as projects when you can afford them. The end result will be a cohesive, coordinated landscape development rather than a piecemeal collection of landscape designs.

What's Involved?

Landscape planning doesn't begin at your local nursery; it begins at home. If you're like everyone else, you are eager to get to work fixing up the old place or relieving the barren look of your new home. But don't let that urge overwhelm your better judgment. There's an orderly planning process that you should follow for best results.

The Process—Four Major Steps. Landscape planning, simply, is determining what you're going to do and how you'll get it done. The complete process includes four major steps: analysis, design,

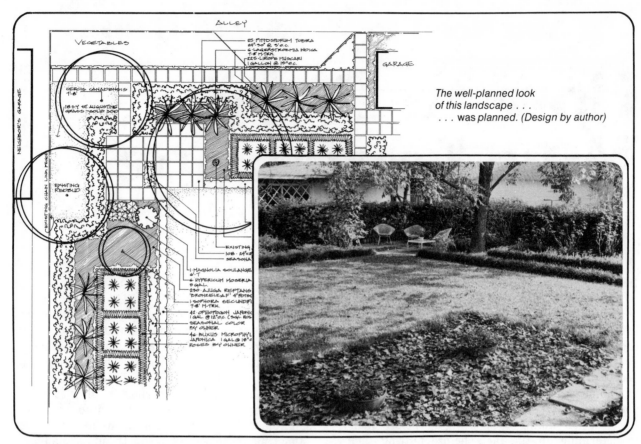

The well-planned look
of this landscape . . .
. . . was *planned.* (Design by author)

installation, and maintenance. All of these steps will be discussed in detail in the next section, but a brief overview at this point might help.

Analysis is the first step in any planning endeavor. In the case of landscape planning, you should analyze yourself and your family, your climate, and your site (residential lot). This involves determining your family's wants, needs, capabilities, and limitations; learning the nature of and all pertinent facts about your climate (regional, local, and on-site); and observing and evaluating your site's possibilities and limitations.

The second major step in the landscape planning process is *designing* the landscape. Here you rely on the specific information and examples in this and other books and upon your own imagination to generate ideas which are realized first on paper and then on the ground. The design should be based on the analysis you've already conducted. After all, that was the whole reason for doing it!

The next step is commonly—and mistakenly— considered the only step: *installation.* Whether you do it yourself or contract it out is a decision that may or may not be easy for you to make. It's a decision largely based on economics, although other important factors must also be considered. More about that later.

The last major step—*maintenance*—usually is not considered a part of the process at all. But the quality of maintenance a landscape receives can largely determine whether or not the original design intent is finally realized. Landscape design, dealing as it does with dynamic, ever-changing materials, is at the mercy of natural processes of change. Through proper maintenance, those processes can be made to work in your favor toward the fulfillment of the design. Since maintenance can so strongly affect the final outcome of a design, it's important for you to fully understand its place in the landscape planning process. Just as important, you must know the kind of maintenance you can afford—in time and money—before you commit yourself to any design.

Planning Considerations. The landscape planning process is the same regardless of where you live. The specific design solutions achieved, however, will vary (or should) because each design problem is generated by a specific set of landscape planning considerations. Although the specifics vary, the general categories of landscape planning considerations are the same everywhere: *people, climate,* and *site.*

Design is for *people,* whether to use or to appreciate for its beauty. In planning your home landscape you must consider not only your family, but the families in your neighborhood. What you do on your property may affect them either

If You Need Professional Help...

Contact a professional landscape architect if you decide that landscape design isn't your bag. The landscape architect's ability to combine specialized knowledge in the fields of art and science qualifies him (or her) to design outdoor spaces using the media of living plants and construction materials.

In many states a professional license, obtained through examination, is required before an individual can practice landscape architecture. Although it's not a legal requirement, most landscape architects have at least a bachelor's degree in landscape architecture from a professionally accredited college or university.

Since the specific abilities of licensed landscape architects can vary considerably from one to the next, it's wise to select carefully. Find out something about the educational background and experience of two or three individuals and look at a few of the jobs they have designed.

The time to discuss fees is after you've selected a landscape architect on the basis of his apparent ability to perform the services you need. In fact, you'll find that most professionals will not quote specific fees if they know or suspect you're "shopping fees." They will, however, indicate their probable method of charging fees for your particular project and may give a general indication of the fee ranges you might expect.

For most residential projects, fees are either charged hourly or as a lump sum amount. If the project is large enough, the fee may be charged as a percentage of the construction cost.

The type of professional landscape architect I have been referring to provides a design service only and neither sells plants nor engages in contracting. There are two other options, however. Many nurseries provide landscape architectural services, as do some landscape contractors, though to a more limited degree than the professional design office. The same method of selection, however, should be applied with these as with the professional who deals only in design. What you need first is a good, sound design that fulfills your needs; and second, the materials and labor to implement the design. No amount of superb materials, dexterous installation techniques, or fancy talk can correct a poor design.

---

physically (modification of their climate) or visually (particularly in front yards), or perhaps in both ways.

It's obvious that you must consider the *climate* in landscape planning. Not so obvious is the fact that climatic conditions fit within a hierarchy of macro and micro conditions, from broad regional conditions all the way down to specific microclimatic differences found on the north and south sides of your house. Since one of the aspects of humanizing the landscape for people is climate control, it follows that the landscape designer must first understand his climatic conditions.

Your *site* is composed of everything on, under, or above the land you own. In addition, off-site influences such as noises and pleasant or unpleasant things to look at must be considered a part of the site factors. Don't forget, total landscape planning deals with everything around you, both inside and outside.

Step-By-Step Landscape Planning Procedure

Landscape planning, to be effective, must be a methodical, step-by-step process. A disciplined approach will not stifle creativity. On the contrary, you'll find that imaginative thoughts are most easily translated into practical ideas within an orderly procedural framework.

The professional landscape architect follows a definite procedure in preparing any type of landscape development plan. The actual sequence of events may vary somewhat depending on the nature of the project and the landscape architect's own way of doing things. Nevertheless, in residential landscape design the steps are roughly the same no matter who is doing the work. The professional, of course, has the advantage of training and experience, and some have developed that nebulous quality called a "good sense of design." Yet by following a logical, orderly process, you can produce results that will surprise you.

The landscape planning procedure presented here is patterned after the one I normally use for most types of projects. You may find it useful for organizing your own efforts toward the successful landscape development of your home. These steps are sequential and should be accomplished in the order given.

1. Prepare a Program

Basic to the landscape development of your home is an analysis of your particular family situation. Involved in this analysis are: (1) the basic facts about your family; (2) what you want and need the landscape to do; and (3) your capabilities and limitations. Collectively, these are called a *program of requirements for development*, or simply a *program*.

A thorough compilation, analysis, and understanding of these basic "givens" can provide that ever-so-difficult-to-find starting point and a clear direction for your landscape development to follow. These program factors tend to become rigid guidelines that begin to determine the basic form of the garden. Though this is not altogether bad, remember that these guidelines are useful only to the extent that they have been carefully prepared and analyzed to eliminate those that are arbitrary and unrealistic. The finished design will be (or should be) a manifestation of the program. So, the program must be carefully thought out with thoroughness and imagination.

As you become more deeply involved in the actual process of designing the landscape, be flexible and try to eliminate those items that too strongly dominate everything else, to the detriment of the total design. For example, a swimming pool that would engulf practically the entire backyard may constitute a poor use of your limited area. Be frank with yourself in assessing whether or not its expected use justifies its extravagant consumption of space.

Family Facts. Take stock first of the basic facts about your family, your possessions and lifestyle. Do you have children? Pets? How many vehicles do you have and of what type (cars, campers, etc.)? Is this a permanent or a weekend home? Do you like to entertain? What objects do you already have that you would like to include? These questions and many more must be answered as a part of your self-analysis (see the KIT at the end of the book).

Don't forget to include future facts—the additions to the family that you already know about (children, animals, a second car, etc.). Reflect on your family's attitudes toward various aspects of home life—outdoor living (at home or somewhere else?), privacy, gardening, the sense of being part of a neighborhood, etc.

Wants and Needs. Next, determine what you want and need in your landscape—a place for outdoor entertaining, a flower or vegetable garden, shade, privacy. Many of these items are logical extensions of your analysis of the facts already compiled about your family. You might also consider psychological effects you'd like to achieve—an enclosed or wide open feeling to the exterior spaces, a look of permanency or seasonal change, etc. Make a list of objects to include—some

favorite plants, a piece of garden ornament, a swimming pool. You need not list your dislikes, since they'll never be brought up for consideration anyway.

Before you finally establish your program, let yourself dream a little. Some of these dreams may go up in smoke once you have completed a preliminary cost estimate, but don't let that possibility stifle your imagination at this point. Be realistic, of course, but allow some room for whimsy!

Capabilities and Limitations. In any do-it-yourself project a realistic assessment of your capabilities and limitations as they relate to money, time, and know-how is essential. Without it you may reach the end of the cafeteria line and discover that your limitations in size of stomach and pocket book far exceed your capabilities of ingesting all the goodies.

The amount of money you can afford to spend right now is relatively fixed, but don't let your current monetary situation stifle creativity. Plan generously but realistically, the way you'd like to see it done ultimately. Then, you can figure out how to accomplish your plan in phases as you can afford them, or determine ways to reduce the cost of the design while maintaining its integrity. A common rule-of-thumb states that a good budget for complete landscape development is between 5 and 10 percent of the cost of the house, not including any special items such as swimming pools, major garden structures and the like. This is only a rule-of-thumb, a place to start in your budgetary thinking. Your development could cost considerably less or considerably more depending on how little of how much you intend to do. The table on page 5 gives an indication of installation costs of typical residential landscape items as an aid to your budgetary planning.

How much time will it take to complete all this planning? How long will it take to complete the installation? The only honest answer I can give is, "Much longer than you think it will!" Landscape planning requires more than a couple evenings, but just how many more depends on the extent of the development you are planning and how easy it is for you to accomplish the various steps involved (know-how). Likewise, the amount of time necessary to perform the installation work depends on the same factors.

Because the time factor is so unknown, it's important for you to approach landscape planning with an attitude of wanting to spend the time necessary to do it right. If you're not prepared to make that kind of commitment, you might as well take this book back to the store for a refund.

(text continued on page 6)

Common Landscape Installation Costs

The intent of these data is to make you aware of the magnitude of cost involved in landscape development and to demonstrate *relative costs* between similar landscape items. Since dollar costs can escalate so quickly in these inflationary times, and since these figures are taken from a specific part of the South, they should not be used in the preparation of a cost estimate. The prices shown include installation by a qualified contractor unless noted otherwise.

Basics

- Grading (rough and fine): $.15-$.20/sq. ft.
- Grading (fine only): $.05-$.10/sq. ft.
- Subsurface drainage:
  6″ diameter plastic (PVC) drain pipe: $7-$10/linear ft.
  8″ diameter plastic (PVC) drain pipe: $8-$12/linear ft.
  12″ x 12″ concrete catch basin with iron grate; $100-$200 each
- Underground sprinkler system (automatic): $1500-$2500 ($.16-$.30/sq. ft.) for an average-sized residential lot. Subtract $400 for a manual system

Surfacing

- Concrete pavement:
  Troweled or broomed finish: $2.50-$3/sq. ft.
  Exposed aggregate (Pea gravel): $3.50-$4/sq. ft.
- Brick pavement (set in mortar on a concrete base): $6-$9/sq. ft.
- Asphalt pavement: $4-$5/sq. ft. (large quantities are much less expensive)
- Iron ore pavement: $.50-$1/sq. ft. (3″ depth)
- Wood deck:
  Redwood: $7-$9/sq. ft.
  Southern Yellow Pine (treated): $6-$8/sq. ft.
- Lawn grass:
  Solid sod (St. Augustine Grass): $.22-$.30/sq. ft.
  Spot sod (St. Augustine Grass, 3″ x 4″ blocks spaced 12″ apart): $.04-$.06/sq. ft. of area
  Seeded (Common Bermuda Grass, hydroseeded): $ .06-$.08/sq. ft.

- Groundcover beds (1-gallon plants spaced 18″ apart): $2-$2.50/sq. ft. of bed area
- Pine bark mulch (3″ depth): $.23-$.26/sq. ft.
- Jute erosion net: $.10-$.15/sq. ft.
- Edger board (2″ x 4″ wood): $2-$2.50/linear ft.

Enclosure

- 6′ Brick wall: $40-$60/linear ft. (varies with price of the brick selected)
- 6′ Wood fence (1″ x 4″ boards, solid): $6.50-$7.50/linear ft.
- 3′ Two rail fence: $4.50-$5.50/linear ft.
- 3′ Railroad tie retaining wall: $6-$7.50/linear ft.

Shelter

Costs are extremely variable. A "typical" residential lath shade structure over a patio could range from $500-$7500, depending on design.

Miscellaneous

- Swimming pool: $10,000-$15,000 (quite variable, depending on features)
- 12-volt lighting kit (six fixtures, wire, transformer): $200 (not installed)
- 120-volt garden fixture: $20-$50 (not installed)
- Greenhouse (varies with size and materials): $700-$5000 + (not installed)

Planting

- 1-gallon shrubs: $3.50-$5
- 5-gallon shrubs: $12-$18
- 15-gallon shrubs and trees: $80-$90
- 1½″ caliper trees (balled-and-burlapped): $60-$80
- 2½ caliper trees (balled-and-burlapped): $90-$130
- 3″ caliper trees (balled-and-burlapped): $190-$220
- 4″ caliper trees (balled-and-burlapped): $350-$400
- 6″caliper trees (machine planted): $500-$650

How much do you know about planting a tree, or preparing a groundcover bed? How about masonry or carpentry? Honest answers to questions like these will save you grief later on.

Another consideration you should not treat lightly is your maintenance capability in terms of both the time and money you are willing to spend. Are you a "dirt" gardener? Do you enjoy gardening for the exercise and sense of accomplishment it gives, or would you rather be sailing? Be very candid with yourself on this point, and don't assume that you'll drastically change to fit the needs of the garden—it will quickly become an albatross. Instead, design the garden to fit your lifestyle.

Consider also what continuing maintenance costs you are willing to bear. These "hidden costs" of landscape development often go unnoticed until that rude awakening (usually at income tax time) when you total up how much you spent last year for lawn fertilizer, insecticides, fungicides, and then wonder how much it must have cost to water the lawn all summer long. Although maintenance costs are difficult to quantify at the program stage of landscape development, their existence can at least be tucked away in the back of your mind (not too far back) for consideration at the design stage.

2. Analyze Your Site and Climate

One of the tenets of current landscape design theory is that the design should emanate from and respond to the nature of the site. To achieve such a design, you must become thoroughly acquainted with your site. No mere once around the house is sufficient if you're serious about developing a quality environment. Be critical. Be thorough. Seek to discover both the good and bad qualities of your site, not only in terms of its physical features, but also in terms of its possibilities and limitations for development. Sensitive, perceptive site analysis, performed with the program factors in mind, can lead you directly into design solutions that are all the more effective because they draw their existence from the site itself.

There is much more involved in site analysis than you might at first imagine. You should be concerned not only with your own parcel of land and everything that's on, under, or above it, but also with the surrounding properties. In addition you should make a thorough analysis of your climate, both immediately on and around your lot and in the broader region of which you are a part. A brief look at each of these aspects of site analysis will give you a better idea of what's involved. For a more detailed listing of what to look for, see the KIT at the end of the book.

The first step toward understanding everything you can about your site is to gather as many existing site drawings as are available to you. The drawings you'll find useful are your deed plat, architectural drawings of your site and house, and a topographic survey of the site. These drawings, along with measurements and notes you make on-site yourself, will be used later to prepare the landscape development plan. Page 85 of the KIT describes the drawings mentioned above and tells where you might find them. The KIT also describes a simple method you'll find useful in measuring your site (page 86). While you're collecting documents, obtain a copy of your subdivision's deed restrictions if you don't already have one. These will affect what you can and cannot do on your property.

The best method of making notes about your site is to put them on a rough sketch of your property. Use the plat or architectural site plan as a guide, and sketch on a sheet of typing paper your property lines, house (including rough locations of windows and doors), garage, driveway, front walk, rear terrace, and other major features like clumps of trees, etc. Don't worry about artistic beauty in this sketch, but do try to keep it neat. Make the sketch large enough to fill up most of the paper, but leave room for notes.

Now you're ready to begin your site analysis. A good place to start is inside the house. Go from room to room and determine which windows have important views and of what. Will the drapes be open most of the time or closed? Observe circulation patterns inside the house and the various possibilities for moving between inside and outside areas.

Continue your analysis outside by observing and making notes about everything on your lot, views outward from your lot, and views of your lot (from the street, neighboring two-story houses, etc.). Note anything you can think of that might relate to the development of your site. Anything you can see, hear, smell, or feel on your property potentially affects its use and/or beauty.

Site analysis also includes observation and analysis of the climate on and surrounding the site. If you have just moved into a climatic region unfamiliar to you, talk with neighbors, the local weather bureau, and county agents to find out the basics of your climate (rainfall amounts and seasons, temperature extremes, most pleasant seasons for outdoor living, etc.).

Within a broad regional climate there are always localized areas that differ from the norm by being hotter or colder, more open to wind, etc. These micro-climates can even be observed within the

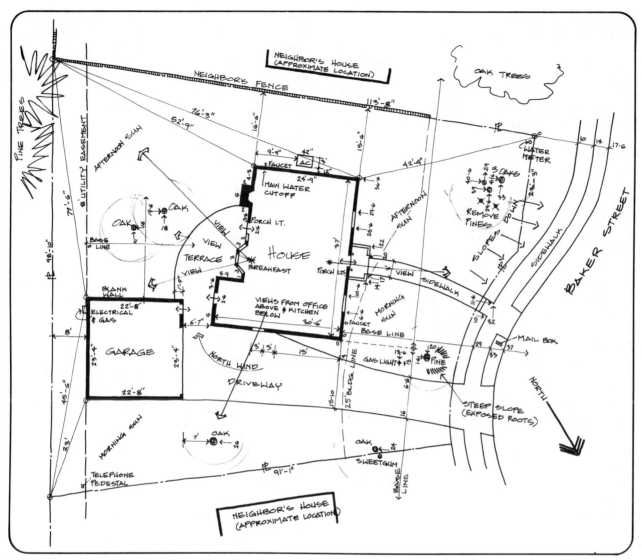

The site analysis and measurement sketch.

confines of your site. For example, certain areas may be shielded from sun or wind because of existing vegetation or because of the orientation and configuration of your house and surrounding houses. If you have lived in the house for a year or more, you probably already know the micro-climatic features of your site. But if you've just bought the house, you can easily deduce most of them by careful on-site observations and by finding the answers to these basic questions: Which direction is north? What are the prevailing wind directions in summer and winter? What are the highest and lowest sun angles at your latitude? (See the KIT.) Don't forget to note all of these facts at an appropriate place on your sketch.

One important aspect of site analysis often overlooked is what might be termed a "character analysis." Every site has a certain feel about it—a certain character—which derives from all of the site features we have been discussing. Your first impressions upon seeing and experiencing the site tell you something about its character. Do you feel welcomed? Do you feel hemmed in by surrounding houses? Can you escape from the sounds of nearby streets? Do you have a feeling of being sheltered by neighborhood trees or is "bald prairie" a more apt description?

Don't rely entirely on what you experience at one given moment; your site's character changes with the time of day, the season, and the weather. If you have time and are patient enough, live with the site for a while and experience it in as many different moods as possible before you begin your landscape planning. With a little imagination, you can determine what the site will be like in those seasons and conditions you have not experienced.

Analyzing Your Site and Climate   7

3. Prepare a Preliminary Plan and Cost Estimate

Having prepared a program and an analysis of your site and climate, you're ready to begin the fun, creative part of the landscape planning process—designing the landscape. Involved in this phase are the preparation of a preliminary plan and cost estimate, and drawing the final plan to be used as a guide for installation. Here's where you muster all of the borrowed ideas you've collected and put them together with your own inspired thoughts into a cohesive design.

Don't just copy what someone else has done. As you most likely discovered in the analysis you just finished, your particular situation is unique. The design you finally achieve must respond to that uniqueness if it is to be all it can be. So if you see something you like, determine why you think it's a good solution for that particular situation, and then apply the principle you've just learned to your own design. Let your design evolve from your own design requirements.

Why Draw Anything? The professional landscape architect puts his design ideas down on paper in the form of a landscape development plan for two very basic reasons. First, this is the easiest and best way to communicate his ideas to the client. In addition, the plans serve as guidelines for transforming the designer's ideas into reality on the ground—in short, they are construction documents.

You too will need drawings to act as construction guidelines for whoever does the installation work. But beyond that, there are many other reasons for drawing landscape plans. If your memory resembles a sieve, as mine does, you'll find it difficult to remember all of your ideas. Sketch them on paper and you'll have all of them to study, evaluate, modify, eliminate, or to generate new ideas. Don't erase or throw any sketches away. The idea you thought wouldn't work may turn out to be the best one after all, perhaps with only a slight modification.

Another practical reason for drawing a landscape plan is that it's much cheaper to practice the trial-and-error process on paper—better to waste a little paper than a lot of time! In a few evenings of sketching you can weed out all the mistakes it would have taken several years to discover had you plunged ahead without a plan.

Putting your ideas on paper makes it easier to visualize relationships of various areas of the yard to each other. Shapes of groundcover beds, pave-

ment, or other areas are more easily studied and refined on paper. In short, doing your planning on paper allows you to completely think through a design solution (or several solutions) for your entire site as a unified whole.

For the homeowner, the value of a drawing, even a crude one, is not so much in the drawing itself but in the *thought processes* its creation requires. To put anything on paper, you must first analyze and then make decisions—you must stop and think.

On the other hand, too much two-dimensional paper planning can make you forget three-dimensional reality. As you draw try to visualize your ideas in three-dimensions. Take your sketches outside and visualize them right on the spot. You might even lay them out on the ground with a hose or a string and some wooden stakes. Then go back to the drawing board and refine the design.

The Base Plan. In order to have something over which to sketch ideas, you must draw a base plan (sometimes called a plot plan or site plan). This is a plan, drawn to scale, of everything that exists on your site. The base plan is so called because it is the base from which you begin your design. The completed base plan is overlaid with transparent sketch paper on which you draw your rough ideas before finalizing them on the final landscape development plan.

It's probably easiest for you to draw the base plan on graph paper with a pencil. If you want to use ink, save that for the final plan. The KIT at the end of the book lists all the drawing materials you'll need. Graph paper marked off at four or eight squares to the inch (¼ inch or ⅛ inch respectively on the paper equals 1 foot on the ground) is the best kind for residential design. The professional landscape architect typically uses plain white drawing paper (available in rolls) rather than graph paper because he uses a "scale" (sophisticated ruler) which is marked off in 1-foot increments at various scales. Graph paper is more practical for the homeowner as it's available in small quantities.

To draw a base plan for your site, you'll need, along with the drawing materials mentioned in the KIT, the sketch you made when you measured the site, your deed plat, architectural site plan, and topographic survey (if you have one). First, draw the property lines and easements. Get the dimensions of these from either the deed plat or architectural site plan, but check the property lines against your own measurements. If your lot is oddly shaped, you may need the help of a protractor and

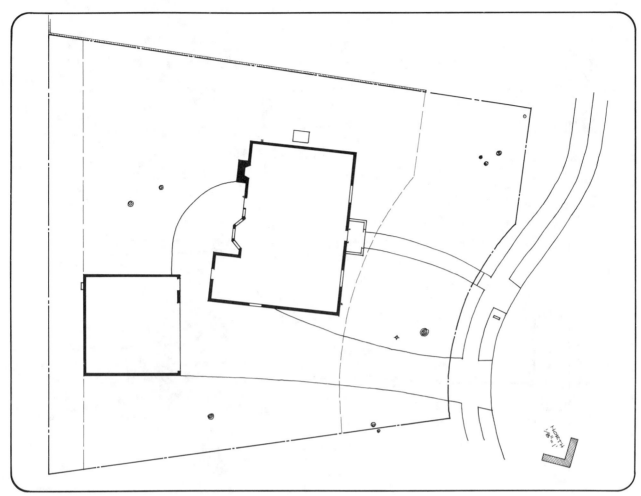

The base plan.

compass to draw it. Page 88 of the KIT suggests some graphic symbols you'll find useful in making your drawing.

Next, draw major items such as the house, garage, other structures, street, walks, driveway, and patio. It's important to locate the house and garage correctly with respect to the property lines. Rely on your own on-site measurements for this rather than the other drawings, because many times the house isn't located exactly as shown on the architectural site plan, and deed plats are notoriously wrong (at least in my experience).

After these major items are drawn, add other miscellaneous items such as trees, light and power poles, air conditioning compressor, etc. If you have a topographic survey, transfer the contours to your base plan. Finish by drawing an arrow showing which direction is north and by indicating the scale of your drawing (¼ inch = 1 foot, etc.).

Data Review. Before you begin designing, it's a good idea to look over the data you've collected so far, particularly if it's been a week or more since you began. Reread the program to refresh your memory as to what you decided you want your landscape to be and to include. Look once again at the sketch you made while measuring your site and read your notes to fix clearly in your mind the problems that must be solved. Review your climatic data and study the existing relationships of areas and objects on your site. Read your deed restrictions to refresh your memory on what you can and cannot do. All this information will begin to suggest possible design solutions for you to explore.

Site Analysis Diagram. You'll find it easier to understand the site factors potentially affecting your design if you make a site analysis diagram. This is merely a rough diagrammatic sketch indicating the major climatic factors affecting the site (prevailing wind, sunny and shady areas, etc.) along with the various site characteristics you discovered during your site analysis (good and bad

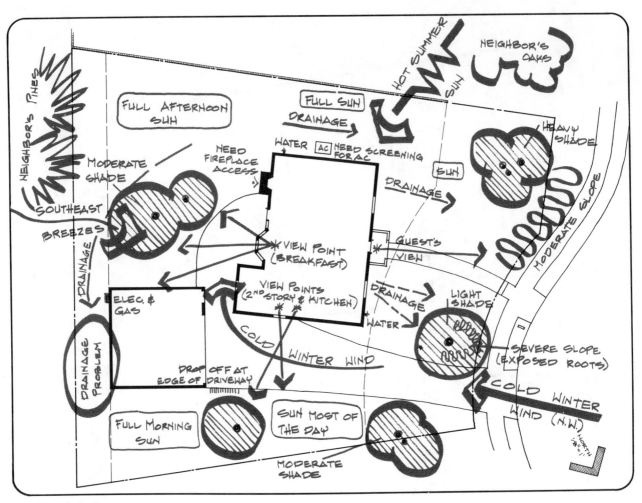

The site analysis diagram.

views, drainage problems, etc.). Use arrows to denote direction, circles to indicate areas, or other similar symbols. This diagram should be made on a sheet of tracing paper laid over the base plan. The information for this diagram is derived from the notes on your site measurement sketch and from your climatic data.

Area Diagram. After completing and studying the site analysis diagram, and with it set aside (but near at hand), place another sheet of tracing paper over the base plan. Since your design should proceed from the general to the specific, begin by dividing your site into areas of usage. Draw circles to indicate where the outdoor cooking and lounging area should be, the children's play yard, the vegetable garden, a greenhouse, etc. Make several diagrams exploring different solutions. As you do, evaluate the relationships of one area to another and to the factors shown on the site analysis diagram.

Once you've accomplished all the suggested analyses, you should begin to see a broad design solution evolving logically from the data. Keep an open mind, however, and don't be afraid to bend your design criteria a little here and there if things don't seem to click. Seldom can you put everything in exactly the right place to satisfy all requirements.

Once you achieve a good solution, neatly sketch it on a sheet of tracing paper. Do all of your sketching freehand at this point.

Detailed Design. Now is the time to begin getting specific, but not too fast. Your strongest tendency will be to get too specific—about exact shapes or precise locations—too soon. Think first in terms of masses and spaces (see page 19) and generalized outlines of surfacing materials (pavement, groundcover areas, etc.). Begin to decide where you need a mass of something to screen a bad view, what that mass should be (hedge, fence,

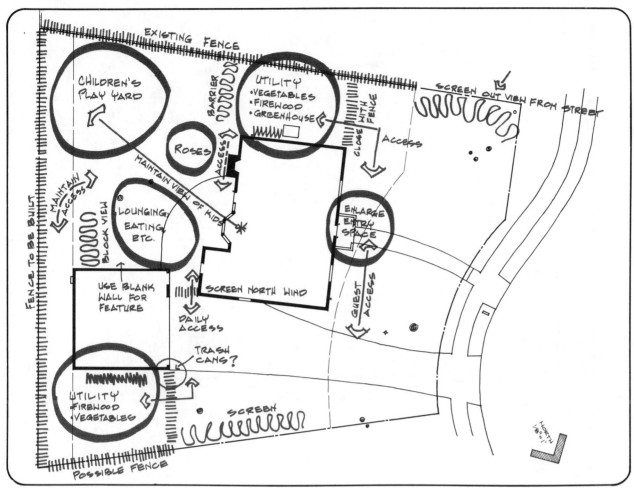

The area diagram.

wall, tall tree), and what kind of space that mass will create. Decide whether you want a tree or a lath structure to provide the shade you've already decided the patio needs and approximately where the tree should go or what size and approximate shape the shade structure should take.

These ideas and many more should be sketched on tracing paper laid over the base plan (draw freehand and loosely). You might even try placing the area diagram over the base plan first as a guide and then sketching on another sheet of paper over that. And don't throw any sketches away (you should see the pile of paper I produce)—you may be able to borrow ideas from one solution to incorporate into another.

Getting started is the hardest thing to do when designing. Those first lines seem hard to come by. But just begin drawing something—doodle! Don't worry about neatness at this point. You can't evaluate the merits of a design if you haven't drawn one. Even if you have only a few blobs on the paper, you can at least say, "That's a dumb thought!" and proceed from there.

Once you arrive at rough solutions for all areas involved in your landscape development, put them all on one sheet of paper. This then becomes a *conceptual landscape plan.* It should show approximate locations and shapes of the major areas of your design. By now you should have decided which general types of surfacings you will use (pavement, grass, groundcover, etc.) and where they will be located. In addition you should know, in general terms, what and where the enclosing elements will be (hedge, fence, etc.) and what kind of sheltering elements you propose and where they will be (trees, shade structure, solid patio cover, etc.).

Completion of the Preliminary Plan. Now you can begin to create specific shapes of groundcover areas or pavement and to decide upon exact locations for trees, shrubs, etc. Remember you are

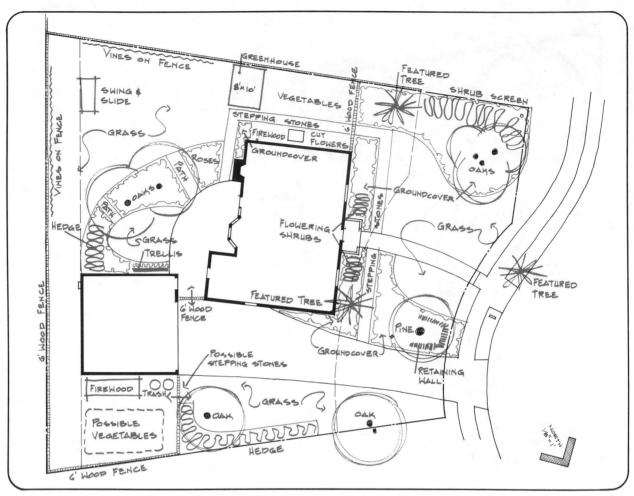

The conceptual landscape plan.

working in three-dimensions and are creating spaces, not paper patterns. Make many sketches on tracing paper over the conceptual plan, with all of this over the base plan. Don't worry, you'll be able to see the base plan because the tracing paper is very thin.

Begin thinking about the specific materials you want to use (brick for the patio instead of concrete, etc.) and how these materials will relate in terms of appearance, function, and maintenance. In some cases it may be easy to select specific materials; in others you may be able to decide only the type that you want and defer the specific decision until you can study the subject more thoroughly. For example, you might decide you want a wooden fence, fairly open, and 6 feet tall. Make a note of that on your sketch and defer the actual design of the fence until you work out other parts of the preliminary plan; but show a specific location for the fence now. Or, you might decide a small flowering tree is what you need for a particular location. If you're

not sure which one to use, you can decide that a little later. Work now on designing the entire yard together.

It would be a good idea, before you go too far, to check with your city or county building division to find out if there are any building code requirements relative to any of the items you're designing. If there are, obtain a copy.

At this point, you're pretty much on your own, guided by your analyses, the design work you've already done, and by your understanding of the design principles and practical suggestions discussed in the rest of this book. That unteachable "good sense of design" enters the picture here, perhaps only as a disguise for common sense.

Once you've created a preliminary plan you're reasonably happy with, draw it neatly on a sheet of tracing paper (still freehand).

Now you can make any specific material selections that you postponed earlier. The KIT at the end of the book contains information you'll find

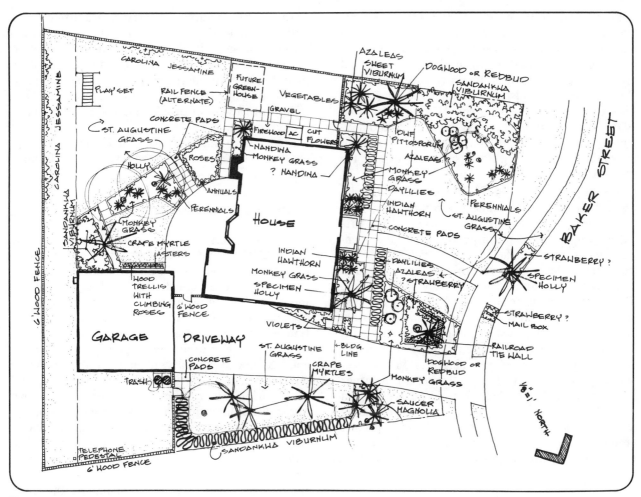

The preliminary plan.

helpful. Remember that these are preliminary selections and are subject to change because of unavailability or high cost, which leads us very nicely to the next subject.

Preliminary Cost Estimate. The time of reckoning has arrived! Through methodical procedures and flights of fancy you have created a plan, albeit a preliminary one. Now it's time to be practical and figure out how much all those great ideas will cost. This isn't a task that can be completed quickly; you'll have to contact many different sources to obtain all the cost data you need. (See the KIT, page 97.) Here's how to go about it:

1. Divide the project into the different kinds of work to be done (concrete paving, wood fencing, planting, etc.). Write these down on a sheet of paper.

2. Decide what work you want to do yourself and what you'll let out to contractors.

3. Determine the quantities of each item of work in the appropriate units (square feet of pavement, linear feet of fencing, etc.).

4. Using the Cost Estimate Worksheet in the KIT, write down the specific items and their quantities.

5. Obtain prices for each item on the worksheet. Those items you are installing yourself will require some detailed figuring of the "nuts and bolts." If you haven't designed an item in enough detail to be able to estimate it that way, do so now. Many how-to-build-it books are available to give you design ideas and show you methods of construction for fencing, pavement, etc.

To obtain prices for contract work, it's best to meet with the contractors to discuss your plan and show them your quantity calculations. They'll probably ask you questions you haven't considered, so be prepared to make some on-the-spot decisions. Don't hesitate to ask for technical advice, but be cautious if they begin to suggest design solutions significantly different from yours. Evaluate these solutions carefully in light of the design criteria you used to prepare the plan in the first place and any new criteria they seem to be suggesting.

6. Once you have obtained the prices for all items on your worksheet, be brave and total them. At this point in landscape planning you must exercise the greatest self-control. Having estimated what your preliminary design might cost, and having picked yourself up from the floor, you reach sorrowfully yet with a great sense of purpose for the eraser—but wait!

It's important to realize, if you don't already, that you've never done anything quite this thoroughly before (if you have, skip this paragraph). You're planning the total living environment of your home. Since you're not accustomed to looking at everything at once, the total cost figure you arrived at probably startled you. But there are ways to get around your apparent inability to afford all that you've designed. Less expensive materials, smaller plant sizes, wider plant spacings, do more of the work yourself—these are some of the ways of reducing the initial cost without significantly altering the design. Another is to accomplish the whole thing in phases, as you can afford it, over a period of a few years, using your plan as a master plan. Divide your project into bite-size chunks in a manner that will create a reasonably completed look at the end of each phase.

Review and Modify the Preliminary Plan. One design technique I've found useful is that of getting away from the trees to look back at the forest. In other words, put your preliminary plan and cost estimate away for a week or so and forget about them. When you get them out again, you'll see good and bad points you missed before—your perspective will have changed.

Take the plan outside and try to visualize what it will look like. Stake it out on the ground and critically observe it. Then get out another sheet of tracing paper and lay it over your preliminary plan. Begin to refine those shapes that still seem a little crude, or shift the location of a tree a little bit to improve a view or provide more shade where it's really needed.

Once you've made whatever modifications seem appropriate, finalize your selection of materials. Note all of these on the preliminary plan.

4. Draw a Final Plan

Earlier I pointed out that one of the reasons for drawing landscape plans was to have construction drawings from which to build your landscape. Now that you have designed your landscape development, you should prepare a final plan that is neat, accurate, durable, and that contains the information you or a contractor will need to do the installation work. Your preliminary plan might be neat enough, but if it's drawn on thin sketch paper which is easily torn, it won't survive rough handling during construction. In addition, your review of the preliminary plan and cost estimate probably revealed changes that needed to be made. These can be incorporated into the final plan along with additional information you did not have on the preliminary plan such as critical dimensions. See the KIT for a list of what to include on the final plan.

The professional landscape architect draws his final plan on white, semi-transparent drafting paper so that multiple copies (prints) can be made by a blueprint company for distribution to the client, contractors, and for his own use in the field; the original drawing thus remains unharmed and available for making additional copies if needed.

Once you've developed some preliminary ideas on paper, stake them out on the ground and try to visualize the finished landscape.

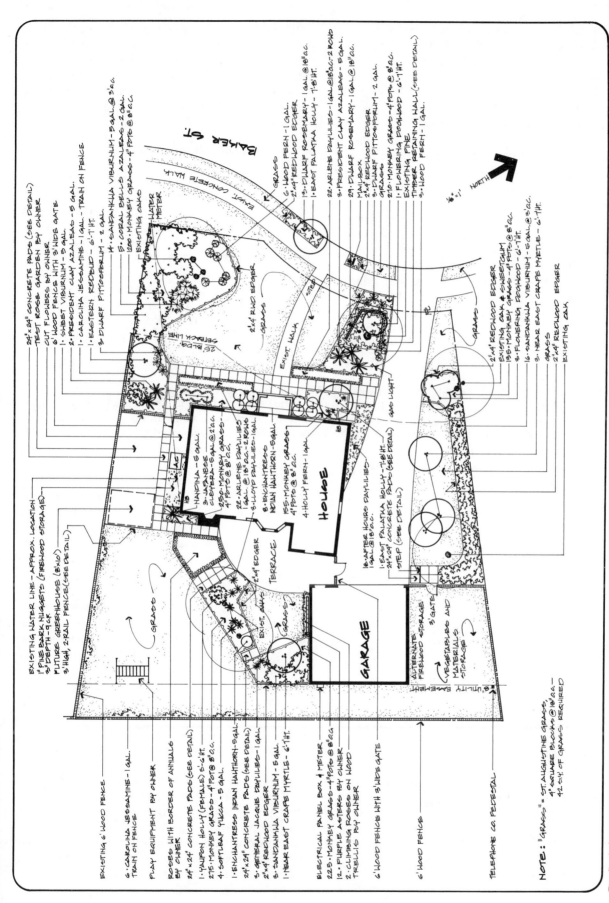

The final plan.

This printing process works only with transparent or semi-transparent papers. Relatively opaque graph papers will not print well (semi-transparent graph papers are available).

This is the ideal approach and one you might want to consider, particularly if you intend to have several different contractors doing work for you at the same time. Otherwise, you can draw the final plan directly on your graph paper base plan, after removing from it those existing items that you've changed (I hope you didn't draw them in ink).

If the preliminary plan is drawn accurately, place the graph paper over it and trace the plan, adding any changes you've made since then. The graph paper is transparent enough if you tape your work to a window before tracing (in the daytime, of course). For permanency, you might consider using ink (permanent ink, of course). If you're afraid you might make a mistake with ink, a dark pencil (#2) will do. A ruler or other straight edge will help with accuracy and neatness of the drawing—important aspects of a final drawing.

If you're doing some of the construction work yourself, such as a wooden shade structure, trellis, etc., you'll find it useful to figure out now a few of the details of how things will fit together, so that you don't waste time and materials during construction. Sketch these details on a separate sheet of plain paper (typing paper works well—not onion skin) so that you don't forget exactly how you planned to do it.

One more item you might find to be a useful part of your construction documents is a list of all the materials you need to purchase—this is often called a "bill of materials." List only those materials you plan to use now. Later phases of the work need their own separate listing.

5. Installation—What's Involved?

Congratulations, you have arrived at the point most people call "landscaping"—rolling up your sleeves and getting to work out in the yard. Now you know the full meaning of the word "landscaping" and why the term "landscape development" seems more appropriate.

Having seen the full scope of landscape planning to this point, you may suspect there's more to the installation of a landscape design than just going out and putting it in. Right! There is much you should know before you turn a spade or spend any money.

Do It Yourself? One basic decision you must make is what work you will do yourself and what you will have contractors do. For the work you do yourself you must have three main things—tools, time, and know-how.

An amateur can do many jobs if he has the right tools. Each type of work (concrete, woodwork, masonry, etc.) requires certain special tools. The investment required may or may not be significant depending on how many different types of work you intend to do yourself. Suffice it to say that the cost of the necessary tools is something to consider.

In the business world, time is money. At home, your time is free of charge; but that's not all there is to the time factor. Be realistic in your assessment of how much time you have to devote to the work you want to do yourself. If you're any kind of a handyman at all, you know that most jobs around the house require much more time to complete than you anticipate. Also, those tasks with which you are the least familiar will take the longest to accomplish. These corollaries to Murphy's Law apply equally well to landscape installation.

The fact that you don't know how to do the work you'd like to do yourself isn't necessarily a handicap if you're a quick learner. Many how-to-do-it books are available just for this purpose. This book, however, is not one of them. Once again, you must be honest with yourself in assessing your ability to handle a particular job.

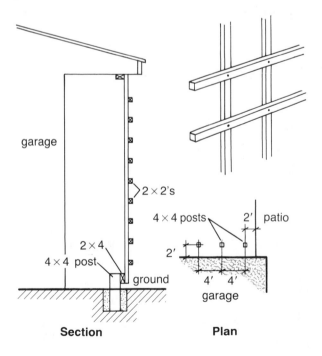

Typical construction detail.

Some of the construction work you'll be doing may require a building permit—check with your city or county building permit department if you're in doubt. In order to obtain the permit, your design must be in conformance with the local building code.

Have it Done by a Contractor? Any work you let out to a contractor will in most cases cost more than if you did it yourself. But if you're careful in selecting a contractor, the quality of work will probably be better. In some cases, you have no choice (swimming pools, for example).

If you have dealt with contractors before, you already know some of the pitfalls involved. For those of you who haven't, here are some tips to help you avoid common problems that may arise.

1. Obtain some sort of contractual agreement. It should clearly state an amount of money due the contractor and, as specifically as possible, the work he will perform and what guarantees he will provide. If the contractor you're dealing with is small and works without a contract, it's a good idea for you to write an informal letter to him enumerating the pertinent information that has been agreed upon. I've run into situations where even friendly relationships with seemingly honest contractors have turned sour through a misunderstanding. Such an informal letter may not hold up in court if not signed also by the contractor, but at least it might help avoid misunderstandings.

2. In some instances you should obtain drawings from the contractor indicating exactly what he will be providing (these are sometimes called shop drawings). Many swimming pool and irrigation contractors do this as a matter of course. For most other work, your own drawings and any written descriptions of work to be performed will suffice.

3. Field design changes almost always occur, particularly on those jobs not well thought out beforehand. During the course of the work any significant changes from what was originally agreed upon should be documented.

4. One of the biggest problems encountered in dealings with contractors is quality control. The best way to solve this problem is to make it clear from the beginning what you will accept and what you won't. Let the contractor know the quality of materials and workmanship you want when you first talk with him so that he can figure his price accordingly. The old adage, "You get what you pay for," is true most of the time.

What Time Of Year? Although all types of landscape installation work can be done any time of year in the South (except on the northern fringes), there are certain factors to keep in mind.

All contractors of the type you'll be dealing with are busiest in the warm, dry months since that's the best time for outdoor work. However, prices are likely to be higher during these peak periods since the contractors are not "hungry" for work. Approach them in the winter off-season and you'll most likely get better prices and a quicker response, although it might take longer to complete the work if the weather doesn't cooperate.

Most people don't think of putting in an irrigation system in the dead of winter, particularly those who have moved to the South from cold northern states. But the best time to plan for the dry summer is before it arrives. In addition, southern winters often have dry spells that make watering necessary. Since the ground doesn't freeze in most southern areas, the water can be used by the plants and will be a welcome relief.

The dead of winter isn't a good time to plant semi-tender or tender plants, but for deciduous trees and hardy plants it's not so bad. Late winter is optimum, since most plants begin root growth about this time in preparation for spring top growth. Also, you shouldn't have any trouble finding a nurseryman or landscape contractor with a little time on his hands before the spring rush.

6. Maintenance—Guiding The Design

It may seem strange to you to think of landscape maintenance as a part of the process of landscape planning. The installation process fits well enough since things always seem to change a little bit from what was planned. But what does maintenance have to do with design? Isn't maintenance basically horticulture?

I've already used the key word: *change.* One of the exciting but sometimes frustrating aspects of a landscape design is that it's a composition of ever-changing elements. In most cases this changing aspect of a landscape must be guided if it is to develop as the designer intended; it must be "maintained." Plants grow and must be artfully pruned to shape them as a sculptor would shape clay, or they die and must be replaced. A tree grows and casts more shade than anticipated requiring a new solution to the planting beneath. Weather changes the color of a stained cedar fence, requiring it to be refinished; the resulting color will be different— what stain should you use? Your children outgrow their play area, freeing it for other uses—what do you do with it now?

Many of these changes in the landscape can be anticipated and planned for, others must be responded to as they occur. In either case, they affect the original design, and so the response to them is properly a part of the planning and design process. But what form should that response take? How do you plan maintenance?

Landscape maintenance is a horticultural subject in its practical aspects, but it is a part of the design process in its effects. While this is not a horticultural book, I do intend to point out to you the specific maintenance considerations inherent in the design of each of the various elements of the garden. These will be discussed in various portions of the following chapters.

Even proper maintenance sometimes fails to guide the landscape to its intended maturity, either because the design was faulty or because uncontrollable (or perhaps unforeseen) factors worked against it. Sometimes, the design just grows old and decrepit. That's the time to grasp the opportunity to freshen things up a bit, to reapply the landscape planning process you've learned, and to once again let the creative juices flow.

Some Basics of Landscape Design

If you have absorbed the previous chapter on landscape planning, you know how to go about creating a landscape development plan for your home—you know the ins and outs of the process. But you must also have a well rounded knowledge of the basic principles and concepts involved in home landscape design, many of which are common to all forms of artistic endeavor. When this body of knowledge and the more specific design suggestions and data of later chapters are combined and applied at the appropriate points in the landscape planning process, the result will be a successful landscape design.

Even though the underlying principles and concepts of landscape design are the same everywhere, design solutions will vary because of many factors, such as budget, location, and taste. It's important to realize that rote conformance to these principles and concepts will not necessarily produce good results. But they must be learned before they can be creatively adapted to a given situation.

Elements and Principles of Design

Landscape design, like most of the other arts, is appreciated largely through visual perception. To understand what we see and the effects it has on us, someone in the dim past organized visual perception into a series of word-concepts representing its many aspects. These have been variously arranged, but the organization presented here seems to be the consensus.

These word-concepts are grouped into two categories: the *elements* and the *principles* of design (or art). These describe more than mere optical effects; they describe an effect on the observer created through involvement of both the eyes and the intellect. Each of these elements and principles has something to contribute to our understanding of the visual world; but a few of them are more significant than the others, and they are the ones that will be discussed here. For a listing of all the elements and principles, see page 20.

The relationship between the elements and principles can be simply stated: The principles are used to create a composition with the elements. In actual practice, however, the composition viewed is the result of a complex interaction of all the elements and principles. This will become clear as we continue our study.

Elements of Design

Space/Mass. Many of the common mistakes homeowners commit in attempting to landscape their homes can be attributed to a lack of awareness of a very basic aspect of landscape design: that it is concerned with the composition of space and mass. The part that mass plays in the landscape is easily observed. Objects in the landscape have varying characteristics of solidity, size, texture, and shape, and all are affected differently by the constantly changing environment.

But the spatial quality of a given landscape is usually not as readily observed, yet it is certainly felt, both emotionally and psychologically, immediately upon entering a space. We feel contained as in an enclosed courtyard, or free as in a rambling estate; oppressed as in a dark, overgrown backyard, or invigorated by a light, airy, open garden.

In approaching the landscape development of your home, think of your property as a chunk of space to be molded and divided into smaller spaces, each with its own character. Just as the house is composed of spaces (rooms), so the garden can be as well, though perhaps not as rigidly. You should realize that as you arrange objects (mass) in the landscape, you are at the same time creating or affecting in some way the spaces between and around the objects; the objects shape the space.

Elements and Principles of Design

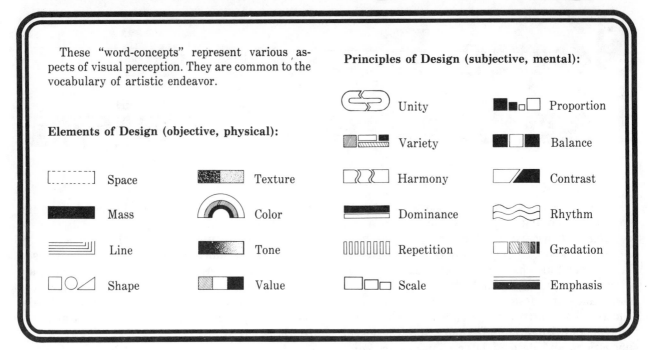

These "word-concepts" represent various aspects of visual perception. They are common to the vocabulary of artistic endeavor.

Elements of Design (objective, physical):

Space   Texture

Mass   Color

Line   Tone

Shape   Value

Principles of Design (subjective, mental):

Unity   Proportion

Variety   Balance

Harmony   Contrast

Dominance   Rhythm

Repetition   Gradation

Scale   Emphasis

Those objects with the greatest visual effect in defining the limits of a space are the ones that extend from the ground to eye level or above and are continuous (fences, hedges, buildings). Other objects within the already defined space affect its nature, the way it feels, as do the dividing or enclosing elements. The quality of the spaces is as important to your appreciation of the landscape as the objects, though you may not consciously realize it.

The significance of the concept of landscape design as spatial design was best expressed by landscape architect James Rose: "[the essence of a garden is] the sense of being within something while still out of doors"—that something is a sensitively designed space. (James C. Rose, *Creative Gardens*, Reinhold Publishing Corp., New York, 1958, p. 22.)

Shape/Line. Everything in the landscape has a shape, including space, as you have already discovered. Generally, we tend to think of shape first as it relates to areas of surfacing—pavement, lawn, groundcover beds—and second as it relates to objects in the landscape. The shape of garden spaces is seldom considered. This is unfortunate since, as we have seen, space is as important as mass in the landscape.

Rectilinear shapes—familiar, orderly. (Design by Glenn Cook)

Angular shapes—movement. (Design by Stanger/Associates)

Circular shapes—a strong visual element outdoors. (Design by Robert F. White and Associates)

The shapes available for use are familiar to everyone. Some of their characteristics—practical, emotional, and psychological—as they relate to landscape design may not be so well known. Let's explore some of these characteristics.

Rectilinear shapes (rectangles, squares) are the easiest to design with. They are the most familiar shapes to most of us since we live with them every day in our homes. Because we associate rectilinear shapes (or any shape incorporating straight lines) with the man-made environment, we tend to think of them as unnatural, and for the most part they are. These shapes instill in us a sense of orderliness, or stability, or compatibility with the built environment.

Modify rectilinear shapes just a little so that they incorporate angles of intersection other than 90 degrees and you've created a different animal. Now, stability gives way to movement in the sense that you feel led in the direction the angled line is pointing. Why doesn't a rectilinear shape invoke this same feeling? It can if the shape is not completely closed; if there is a mysterious opening in one side leading to the unknown. The unexpected presence of an angled line or the mystery of what's

just beyond the opening in the rectilinear shape subconsciously invoke curiosity; thus they generate movement, either visual or physical. Care must be exercised in using angular shapes, however, as an overabundance of different angles becomes muddled and incomprehensible. Even too much of the same angle can be unpleasant if there's no strong reason for the angle to be there in the first place or if it leads to a dead end.

Circles have a sense of completeness about them which is both an observed effect and a psychological, poetic one (the wedding band, turning full circle, etc.). The absence of "hard" angles or corners imparts to circular shapes a softness unobtainable with rectilinear or angular shapes. Though there is the hint of nature in the perfect circular form, there is still a certain artificiality about it. Circles are very commanding shapes when seen in the landscape because the perfection they display is not expected outdoors. They must therefore be used carefully and in moderation. Circular shapes provide as good a sense of enclosure as do rectilinear ones, but they lack the sense of directional orientation we need to be most comfortable.

Elements of Design   21

Free-form shapes—the simpler the better.
(Design by Ross Palmer)

Beyond the pure shapes already discussed, there are, of course, many possible combinations that can be successfully used. These are too numerous to mention in this limited discussion. But there is one other shape that should be mentioned—a shape composed of multiple curves commonly referred to as "free form." This is the shape most often used by unskilled designers, and yet it is one of the most difficult to use properly.

The difficulty lies in the fact that man sees order most easily in familiar shapes, and that most free form shapes are anything but familiar or orderly. James Rose put his finger on the problem when he observed that, "The painfully corseted lady who put a kimono over her corset to 'loosen things up a bit' is similar to what passes for free form today. It is completely free in that its form has nothing to do with what is inside." (James C. Rose, *Creative Gardens*, Reinhold Publishing Corp., New York, 1958, p. 22.) For that matter, it usually has nothing to do with what's outside either. Free form tends to become no form—an amorphous blob dropped from the sky.

The use of free forms seems to derive from a desire to imitate nature or at least to create something "kind of natural." This noble desire is a bit misplaced in its belief that a little spot of nature in the middle of a manicured lawn can be anything but contrived. Hence the reason for the failure of the tree muff (small area of planting surrounding a tree) or the wavy-edged flower bed. The fact that there's more to nature than curved lines doesn't seem to be understood. The curving line can, indeed, be restful, or suggest movement (similar to angular lines), or evoke a feeling of naturalness. But even the pure, crisp, curved line is seldom found in a natural arrangement of things where the relatively ill-defined edge is the norm.

For the dyed-in-wool free form designer, simplicity is the rule to follow. In other words, utilize long sweeping curves, keeping to a minimum the back and forth undulations that complicate the shape.

As this discussion has shown, it's impossible to talk about shape without referring to lines. Any shape has as its defining edge a line. But line exists in the landscape in a more abstract sense, too. For example, a row of shrubs or trees creates a line. When a line of whatever type is well-defined and clearly seen, it has the characteristic of direction—it causes the eye to move along it to its end. A complex, contradictory grouping of lines confuses one's directional sense, whereas one or several lines all leading in one direction reinforce it. This characteristic of lines can be used to advantage in focusing one's attention on a piece of sculpture, a fountain, or a pleasant view, or in forcing people to move in a certain direction. If overlooked, it can visually disrupt a design and destroy any cohesiveness (unity) it might have otherwise had.

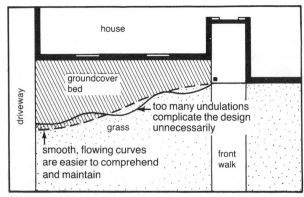

Free forms shouldn't be too free. Maintain order with simple curves.

The directional characteristic of lines can be put to good use. Here, Monkey Grass borders lead the eye to the center of attention, an auxiliary seating area set apart from the main terrace. (Design by author)

Principles Of Design

Unity. The need for order is basic in humans. From complexity we constantly strive to perceive unity or to create it where none seems to exist (grouping stars into constellations, for example). Without unity, man is unsettled, restless, uncomfortable, frustrated.

Often a new term is best explained by its synonyms. Such is the case with the word *unity*, even though it seems understandable enough. In terms of their relevance to landscape design, the most descriptive synonyms are: cohesion, consistency, completeness, oneness, concord, harmony. What I'm suggesting is that a unified landscape design is one in which the whole is greater than the parts, a goal which can only be accomplished if all of the parts work together, are harmonious and consistent in some aspect.

I know of only one way to achieve unity of design, and that is through repetition of the same or similar elements throughout the design, whether they are objects, shapes, materials, colors, textures, lines, or spaces. Generally, it is necessary to repeat more than one of these elements. Unity through repetition may be achieved visually by actually seeing the elements repeated. Or, it may be achieved through the memory of the observer who sees something he remembers having seen or experienced in another part of the garden. Many other means of achieving unity of design have been suggested by others, but if you look closely at them all, you'll find they are rooted in this one concept of the necessity for some common element or elements to be found throughout the design.

When I speak of repetition, I don't mean endless rows of the same shrub, nor do I mean a helter-skelter arrangement of one kind of tree. I'm speaking essentially of "variations on a theme." In order for unity of design to be possible, there must be a dominant "theme" (character, motif) throughout; a thread or several threads that hold things together. This theme becomes the common denominator around which the design is built. For example, a design using rectilinear shapes of different sizes, with wood as the major material in decking, retaining walls, and fences, has a good start toward being unified. Even subtle things like reddish tints of foliage, if repeated in several parts of the garden, can contribute to unity.

Within a unified design there is ample room for variety, and therefore interest, to occur. In fact, variety is necessary to prevent monotony—what you might call too much unity. If carefully designed, the thematic material itself can provide the variety. For example, rectilinear shapes used as a theme could be endlessly modified and combined to create as much variety as desired. Or, an element that contrasts with the theme could be introduced for variety and to strengthen, by comparison, the desired effect. For example, straight lines and curves, when used together strengthen each other by contrast. One element must clearly dominate, however, or disunity will result.

Variety is the principle of design which falls at the opposite end of the spectrum from unity. Just as too much unity is monotony, too much variety is chaos. Chaos, unfortunately, is what typifies much of current residential landscape design today, both amateur and professional. It's easier for the do-it-yourself designer to maintain unity of design by using only a few different elements properly. The difficulty increases as the number of different elements increases. However, it's possible for a design with only three different elements (plants, for example) to be chaotic if the elements are the wrong ones for the particular situation or if they are poorly arranged. On the other hand, 30 different elements, well selected and arranged, could produce a unified design. Beware of arbitrary rules that say you should use only four or five different plants if you want to be successful—it just isn't that simple!

Your tendency will be to concentrate too quickly on details—the various parts of the design. The result will be a collection of objects instead of a unified design—chaos. Seek first to establish a solid framework or structure to the design—a common denominator or theme—and then add the enrichment of harmonious variety.

Scale/Proportion. These two terms are often confused. But understanding them and their importance in landscape design is not difficult when they are discussed together.

The term *scale* refers to a system of grouping units into a series of graded steps according to size, quantity, etc. The first type of commonly understood scale that comes to my mind is the eight-note musical scale—do, re, mi, fa, so, la, ti, do. If one note is missing, disunity results. If a note is out of place, it may be said to be "out of scale" in relation to the other notes—again, disunity results, and you can hear it.

Scale relationships in the landscape are visual and usually are concerned with sizes and quantities. An object in a landscape design is said to be "in scale" if it bears a logical, pleasingly proportioned relationship to the landscape space and to the other objects in that space. This scale relation-

ship may deal with the overall size of the object or the size of its parts (large or small leaves, etc.), or perhaps both. For example, the large-leaved Southern Magnolia may seem out of place in a very small courtyard because of its large leaves. In a larger park-like setting, it would seem more fitting. In one instance it's out of scale, and in the other it's in scale.

Proportion enters the scene as a part of scale relationships. While scale refers to a *series* of graded units, proportion is the comparative relationship *between* the units with respect to size, quantity, etc. A "pleasing" proportional relationship is difficult to define, but it usually means that sizes, quantities, etc., are similar, or at least not grossly dissimilar.

To see how scale and proportion are inextricably combined, take a look at a typical front yard. In most instances the front door entry area is out of scale with the street scene; that is, the proportional relationship of the size of the front porch space to the street scene is unpleasant because the two are so dissimilar in size, with no intermediate-sized elements. There is no *gradation* in size of spaces. The solution can only be to change the proportional relationship by increasing the size of the front entry space and/or creating an intermediate-sized space.

A common mistake in landscape design is using indoor scale relationships outdoors. The problem is that outdoor spaces are usually larger and demand a larger set of scale relationships. In the landscape, objects such as plants must be placed farther apart, dimensions of common items such as steps must be enlarged, and quantities must be increased to produce the same pleasing proportional relationships that were accomplished indoors on a smaller scale.

One problem peculiar to landscape design is the changing scale and proportional relationships of the plants as they grow. Unless you use mature plants, the initial relationships will most likely be poor. But the plants in a well designed and maintained landscape will, in a few years, begin to develop more pleasing relationships to each other and to the surrounding spaces. If well planned, these relationships will continue to be pleasant, though certainly different, at maturity.

To a certain extent there is within each of us a sense of right and wrong proportions, generated mostly by a sense of what feels *balanced*. Our sense of balance is unconsciously governed by our personal understanding of how gravity affects unbalanced objects. This sense of balance and proportion develops in childhood. I once watched a young

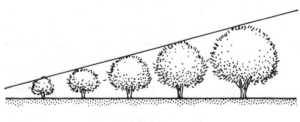

this plant is out of scale: too large and coarse

A graded scale of objects.

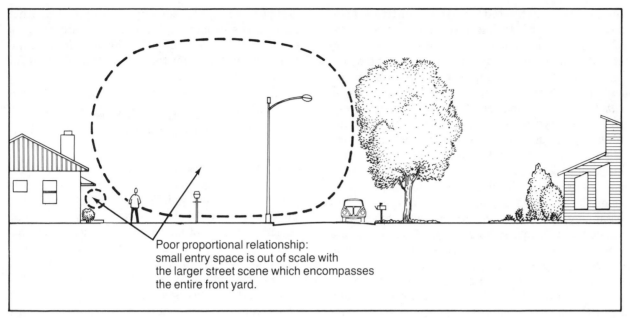

Poor proportional relationship: small entry space is out of scale with the larger street scene which encompasses the entire front yard.

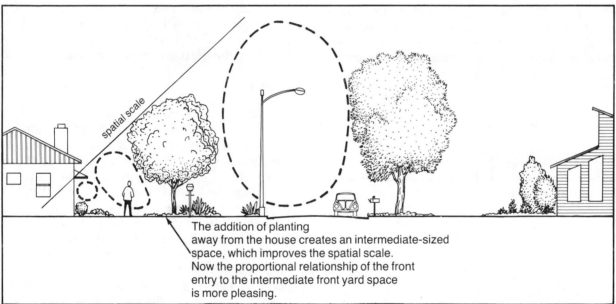

spatial scale

The addition of planting away from the house creates an intermediate-sized space, which improves the spatial scale. Now the proportional relationship of the front entry to the intermediate front yard space is more pleasing.

Scale and proportion illustrated.

boy making a space ship out of toy building bricks. After he had built the body and wings he added the cockpit area (all very futuristic, of course). He stacked brick on top of brick until he reached a point at which he quickly removed the top brick he had just placed—his sense of proportion told him he had built it too tall.

Balance. Quite often I hear this term used by homeowners to describe what they feel is a necessary attribute of good landscape design. Most often what they mean by balance is bilateral symmetry—the same thing on each side of a central axis. While this type of symmetry certainly is balanced, too often it also becomes static and uninteresting. In the hands of talented landscape designers bilateral symmetry can be used effectively to create grand designs, such as in the gardens of Versailles and in many fine southern mansion gardens. It's generally on the scale of the small residence, however, that bilateral symmetry tends to slip toward the sterility and lack of imagination exhibited in the multitudes of southern front yards that have a tree in the middle of each side of the yard with a narrow border of Monkey Grass along each side of the front walk.

A better understanding of this design principle can be achieved if we substitute the word *equilibrium* for balance. Now we can get away from stereotypes and concentrate on creating interesting designs while at the same time maintaining the sense of visual stability that humans require to feel comfortable. Equilibrium of design is achieved through the visual balancing of the masses of the various parts of the design—that is, the balancing of a large quantity of small things here against a few large things over there; or a few strongly textured shrubs here against many less heavily textured plants there; and so on.

This asymmetrical balancing of quantity against size, strength of color against quantity, height against width, is really only another facet of the scale/proportion discussion we just finished. For a sense of equilibrium is achieved in landscape design when the proportional relationships are pleasing—when the visual "weight" of one part of a

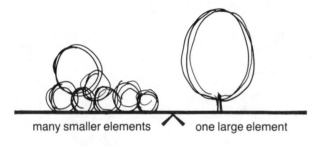

many smaller elements — one large element

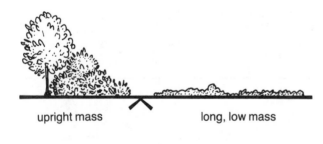

upright mass — long, low mass

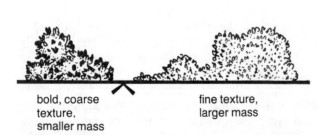

bold, coarse texture, smaller mass — fine texture, larger mass

Asymmetrical Balance. In each illustration, the left side is visually balanced with the right side, even though the two sides contain different elements.

design is similar in some way to that of another part of the design. Asymmetrical equilibrium of design certainly doesn't offer the only design solutions, but it does offer the greatest possibilities for variety and interest.

Characteristics of a Successful Landscape Design

All homeowners have their own reasons for wanting to landscape their homes and, to a certain extent, their own individual ideas of what they hope to achieve. I believe a careful analysis would reveal that most of us want the landscape development of our home grounds to match as closely as possible a fairly standard set of characteristics, the proper combination of which produces what I would call a "successful landscape design." These characteristics are beauty, comfort, convenience, minimum maintenance, flexibility, and safety. Does your proposed landscape design have these characteristics? If so, you've probably succeeded in attaining the goals you've set for yourself.

Beauty

Certainly, everyone wants their home grounds to be beautiful. But achieving the desired results involves more than just adding beautiful things to the yard. It's as much a result of the way things are put together as it is of the intrinsic beauty of the things themselves. Indeed, even mundane objects used in an imaginative way can contribute to a beautiful design. This idea is expressed well by Nan Fairbrother in her book *The Nature of Landscape Design*: "A collection of choice plants is not a landscape any more than a list of choice words is a poem. The merit is in the design, not the material it is expressed in, and the best designs, like the best poems, make ordinary material significant by its arrangement." Although beauty is to some degree defined differently by different people ("beauty is in the eye of the beholder"), you'll have a greater chance of creating a beautiful landscape if you apply the elements and principles of design already discussed.

Comfort—Control of Climatic and Environmental Extremes

The extent to which you use your outdoor spaces for recreation, entertaining, etc., will depend in part on your success in controlling the harsh aspects of the climate and environment. Each step you take to control and modify these conditions will increase the number of days you can use your outdoor spaces in relative comfort. Of course, there will always be periods when just being outside is unpleasant; but even these times can be tempered somewhat through careful planning and design.

Begin by identifying the problems, or potential problems, and the desired results. If you properly execute the first step of the landscape planning process, the preparation of a program, you'll know what activities your landscape is to accommodate (outdoor living, recreation, lounging, etc.). A little thinking will help you identify those climatic and environmental factors most detrimental to the greatest enjoyment of each activity. For example, bright, hot summer sun and strong winds are unwelcome in an outdoor eating area.

Climate Control. The climatic factors to be dealt with are temperature, sunlight, rain, humidity, and wind. Translate these into the extremes that make life outdoors unpleasant and the list of factors to be controlled looks like this: heat, glare, cold, rain, humidity, and strong winds.

In attempting to achieve comfort outdoors, it is often true that modification of one of these factors in turn causes the modification of another. You'll soon see this as you read on.

In most southern climates summer heat is the major source of outdoor discomfort. Coupled with heat is the glare of bright sunlight reflected from pavement and walls. Heat and glare cause problems indoors as well. For example, heat radiating from unshaded pavement near the house can increase the load on your air conditioning system and cause a great imbalance in comfort from one room to the next. This is particularly true if there are many windows near the paved area.

The glare of reflected light may or may not be a problem in your case. If the glare interferes with a good view, it's a problem. On the other hand, the reflected light may be welcome if it is needed to help lighten an adjacent dark room.

Control of heat and glare begins with a knowledge of the directions from which the sun will be shining at various times of day and at various seasons (see the sun angle diagrams in the KIT at the end of the book). Identify what the sun's location will be at the particular times of day you most need the protection. This will help you determine what types of elements you need to block all or part of the sun—trees, shade structures, fences or walls, portions of your house or garage, a neighbor's house or garage—and will also tell you where to locate them.

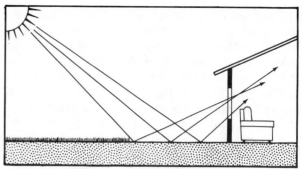

problem: reflected heat and light (glare)

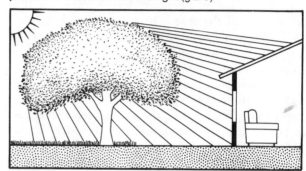

solution: block summer sun . . .

. . . but allow winter sun for warmth

A successfully designed landscape also takes advantage of other elements that provide physical or psychological cooling. Here are some of them:

1. A non-heat-absorbing surfacing such as wood decking could be used.
2. Glare, but not heat, is much diminished on brick pavement.
3. Summer breezes can help cool an area if it is located to adequately utilize them.
4. Water sprayed into the air or onto pavement can physically cool an area, at least temporarily.
5. Plants add moisture to the air through a process called transpiration and thus can contribute to the total cooling effect.

For thousands of years, garden designers in hot, arid climates have been taking advantage of the psychological cooling effect of the presence of water. Whether in placid pools or turbulently flowing streams, water connotes coolness. So strong is this effect that even a small basin can produce it.

At the opposite end of the spectrum is the problem of outdoor comfort in winter. If you're not careful, you may find that the elements serving to reduce the heat and glare of summer are also increasing the cold of winter. Trees located to shade an area in summer should be deciduous if the area is intended to be used also in winter or if it's near the house. Shade structures could have removable panels to allow winter sun to penetrate. On the other hand, if the area is properly located in relation to the sun's position at different times of year, the elements that shaded it in summer may no longer do so in winter.

Other solutions contributing to reduction of cold and thus to greater winter comfort are the blocking of cold winter winds, the use of heat-absorbing and radiating pavements, and a good old-fashioned fire built in a fire pit.

Strong winds are unpleasant whenever they occur. Proper placement of trees, shrubs, fences, and walls can materially reduce or eliminate the problem. But be careful not to eliminate the cooling summer breezes as well. You can only achieve proper placement of blocking elements if you first know the primary direction from which the winds will blow, at all seasons. For more on the subject of wind control, see the discussion of enclosures on page 54.

Rain can only be controlled with a solid overhead cover. If this type of structure over a patio area is not in keeping with other more important criteria you've established, forget it. Just run inside while it rains, or get wet if you prefer!

Humidity also is very difficult to control. Low humidity can be increased somewhat through the use of vegetation and pools of water, both of which will add free moisture to the air. High humidity is virtually impossible to change directly. You'll have better results in both cases by concentrating on controlling and utilizing sun and wind to modify the effects of humidity.

Control of Environmental Factors. In many parts of the South enjoyment of the outdoors is made difficult during warm months by a most formidable foe: the mosquito. Although the protective measures that can be taken against this nuisance are few and not totally effective, they are worth considering if you want to realize the maximum usage and enjoyment from your landscape.

Nature itself can assist you if you locate the outdoor living areas so that breezes blow across them.

Don't rely on breezes alone, though, for they only discourage some of the pests. Other solutions, such as the screening of a porch or gazebo, are more effective. Various types of electric bug killers and attractants will also help by drawing the bugs away from the area of usage.

One of the major environmental problems today is the triple-whammy of air, noise, and water pollution. Of these, air and noise pollution are the two most likely to be encountered at home. Both can be only mildly tempered in the outdoor home environment.

One of the primary modifiers of air pollution for the homeowner is vegetation, principally trees. For a discussion and list of pollution-resistant trees, see *Trees for Southern Landscapes*, by William D. Adams, Pacesetter Press/Gulf Publishing Co., Houston, Tx., 1976. Trees serve to physically collect dust on their leaves before it can settle to the ground. In addition, a canopy of foliage over your outdoor use areas will protect against sun and possibly wind.

Plants absorb many of the pollutants fouling the air and give off fresh oxygen in return. However, this effect is significant only when large quantities of vegetation are present. For example, a row of shrubs along the front of the house will do little by itself to modify the surrounding atmosphere.

Control of noise pollution at home is even more difficult. The subject is complex and has been studied scientifically with varying and conflicting results. Nevertheless, there are a few things you can do to reduce noise levels.

Solid walls, fences, and the house itself are the most effective noise buffers. These primarily deflect the sound, sometimes into another part of the yard. Locate the areas most sensitive to noise so as to take advantage of these buffers. Plants also can be utilized to both absorb and deflect

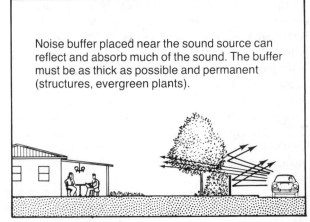

Noise buffer placed near the sound source can reflect and absorb much of the sound. The buffer must be as thick as possible and permanent (structures, evergreen plants).

Control of noise pollution.

sounds. The buffering effect increases as the plants are placed closer to the source of the sound. However, in the typical residential situation the leeway for locating the buffer is usually not great, and the results will differ little from one location to the next.

Convenience

A landscape design that is not arranged for convenient usage will not be fully used and thus cannot be termed successful. Convenience in the garden comes in several forms. First, garden areas must be so located with respect to each other and to the various areas inside the house that the desired activities can be carried on easily. For example, an outdoor eating area should be easily and quickly accessible to the kitchen. A play yard should gain access other than through a lounging area.

The detailed design of the garden can also have much to do with how convenient it is to use. For example, gates should be wide enough to allow passage of garden carts and lawnmowers; stepping stones should be spaced to make walking easy.

Minimum Maintenance

The statement I hear most consistently in my conversations with clients is, "I want low maintenance." This seems to be the universal ideal in all residential landscape design. Minimum maintenance designs certainly can be created, but they are usually more expensive to install since they involve more construction and less planting (pavement instead of grass, fencing instead of hedges, etc.). Also, as the money, time, and skill available for maintenance decreases, so must the careful attention to design increase. Entire books have been written on the subject of low maintenance garden design, and these should be consulted for more detail than can be included here.

Since most construction materials, such as brick, concrete, and wood, require very infrequent maintenance to be kept in good condition, the subject of designing for minimum maintenance deals mostly with plants. If you make your plant selections fit the climate, existing horticultural conditions, and the intended size and use of the area, you'll have solved a large portion of your maintenance problems before they occur. For example, shrubs that outgrow the space provided for them must be constantly sheared back just to maintain the status quo. A properly selected shrub can be allowed to grow to its natural mature size within the space allotted to it. The more maintenance you want to eliminate, the more the natural processes must be allowed to operate.

Many times the use of plants native to your area will help reduce maintenance because they are supposedly adapted to your conditions. This is true only if the plants are placed in an environment much like their native one with respect to soil, sun, water and wind exposure. Unfortunately, many potentially useful native southern species are not widely available, although a diligent search will usually turn up at least one nursery in your area which handles some of them.

Grouping of plants according to horticultural requirements is another way to produce better results with less effort. It is much easier to water an entire plant bed according to the same schedule than to water some plants now, other plants in a few days, etc. The problem usually becomes self-solving, since the plants not suited to the level of maintenance they are receiving simply die.

The style of design you create can have much to do with the level of maintenance required. Very formal gardens usually require much hedge shearing and general trimming, mowing, edging, raking, etc., to keep them neat and geometric. Naturalistic gardens, on the other hand, need not be so highly maintained to produce the desired effect.

Flexibility

In the world of landscape design, change is as inevitable as death and taxes. To be successful over any extended period of time, a design should be able to respond to change in a manner that leaves it intact, though perhaps different. Attempting to keep a design the same forever as if in a museum is both an unrealistic goal and a very dull one.

Change manifests itself in many different forms. Daily changes occur in lighting patterns and temperatures. Seasonal changes include variations in sun angles, temperatures, rainfall, and foliage coloration. Physical changes in construction materials caused by weathering and use are slow but sure. Plants grow and die.

Family needs and desires also change over the years. There may be a need for more parking space for the third car or a new boat. Children outgrow their play areas, leaving them to be converted to some other use; or perhaps the children have reached the age when it's time to put in a swimming pool.

As you design, think of the future to ensure flexibility. When the sand box under the tree in this children's play area is no longer needed, it can be turned into a groundcover bed, a small patio area, or an extension of the work area for the adjacent tool shed, whichever use is most needed at the time. (Design by author and owner)

This changing aspect of the landscape is one of the exciting things about it, but it necessitates close attention to design. Response to change must begin even before the change itself—that is, at the design stage. Careful attention to the preparation of a program can help you foresee the potential for change in the various parts of the design and allow you to plan for it.

Much of the response to change must come in the form of continuing maintenance (replacement of dead materials, repainting, etc.). However, a well designed landscape will change with a minimum requirement for maintenance. Suffice it to say that a flexible landscape design is one that grows better as it grows older.

Safety

The creation of a landscape design that provides safe conditions for outdoor activities results mostly from logical, careful thought at the design stage. Most potentially hazardous conditions can easily be eliminated before they occur.

Here are some of the common danger points to watch for:

1. The juncture of driveway and street: Any vision obstructing plantings will cause an obvious problem. Plants that grow taller than about 3 feet can create an unsafe condition.

2. Abrupt changes of elevation such as steps, walls, or edges of wood decks: People must be made aware that the change of elevation is there, either by use of protective rails, night lighting, or by other means. In the case of steps, proper design will make their use comfortable and safe. Very low, single steps in an otherwise flat pavement are unexpected and usually trip people.

3. Children's play area: Avoid low-hanging objects, sharp corners, and splintery wood.

4. Swimming pools: Fencing is a necessity to prevent small children from accidentally gaining access when no one else is around.

5. Vegetation: Plants that attract bees or that have many dangerous thorns do not belong next to doors or other areas where people cannot avoid them. Very poisonous plants obviously do not belong in play areas for tots, or any place to which small children have free, unsupervised access.

Other Important Design Concepts

In any logical, organized discussion of a complex subject, there always seem to be a few topics that must be explored but that can't be fitted into the framework. Rather than burden other chapters with them, I've chosen to collect them in this section in a series of essays.

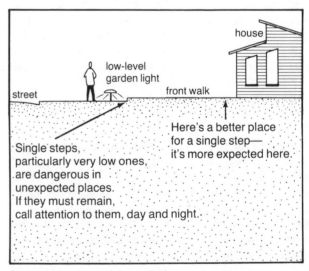

Be conscious of safety as you design.

Visual Effects

In the realm of visual perception, not everything is as it appears to be—the eye is easily fooled (optical illusions). This quirk in our nature can be used to advantage by employing various design techniques (tricks, if you prefer) to create a certain desired effect. Here are some examples:

1. As objects in the landscape increase in distance from us, they appear smaller, less distinct and, if the distance is great enough, lighter in color. This visual principle can be utilized to help avoid diminishing the apparent size of an already small space. For example, small-leaved, light-colored plants, or fences with narrow boards placed at the limits of a space will help produce this effect. On the other hand, large-leaved, dark-colored plants and fences with wide boards tend to make the small space seem even smaller.

2. An object in the landscape will seem farther away if the view of the object is slightly broken up (by open shrubs, trees, screens, etc.). The reason is that the true distance cannot be fully observed and the object is visually broken into smaller units, thus making it apparently recede.

3. The narrowing of a space at the distant end will create a false sense of perspective and make the space appear longer than it is. This can be done with hedges, fences, or rows of objects (trees, brick columns, etc.). This effect is more difficult to create in smaller than in larger spaces.

There are also other visual effects you can produce that do not involve fooling the eye. For example:

1. A scene in bright light viewed through a dark area such as a dark archway or the deep shade of a tree will be emphasized because of the strong contrast. In effect what happens is that the view is "framed" by the darkness, thereby having attention focused upon it. This is a common effect you see everyday through the windows of your house, the room being darker than the view through the window.

2. Focusing attention on an important view can also be accomplished in other ways as well. The directional nature of the lines of a path, hedge or fence, etc. can be utilized to point to the center of attention.

3. The relationship of foreground to distance is always important but particularly so in scenes meant to be viewed from only one vantage point. It is possible for objects in the foreground, though

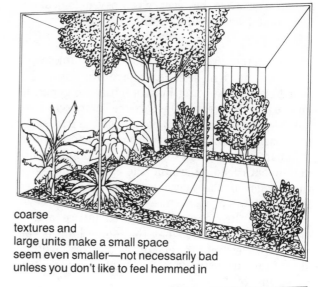

coarse
textures and
large units make a small space
seem even smaller—not necessarily bad
unless you don't like to feel hemmed in

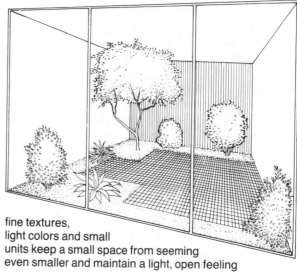

fine textures,
light colors and small
units keep a small space from seeming
even smaller and maintain a light, open feeling

When designing small spaces, you may need to use a few visual tricks.

small, to visually overpower more distant but larger ones either by physically blocking the view or by being so strong in color or other feature that they are distracting. This can, of course, be used to advantage if the view is unpleasant.

These examples are all rules-of-thumb, and as with all rules of this sort, the designer must realize that there are exceptions.

Psychological Effects

I suppose a book could be written on the various aspects of the landscape and the psychological effects they have on us. Most would probably be so obscure and abstract as to be of no real value in design. There are, however, a few psychological effects that I have found useful to create.

1. Humans are curious about the unknown. Japanese garden designers have for centuries relied on this aspect of human nature to generate and sustain interest in the garden. Their technique has been to reveal only a portion of the garden to the observer from any one viewpoint and to make it apparent that there's more just around the corner. A path leading around the end of a hedge or the corner of the house beckons the curious to follow it to its conclusion. A tantalizing glimpse of something through a vine-covered lattice makes one want to see just what that something is. Be sure, however, that the end of the path or the other side of the lattice really is worth the effort to see, a real climax.

2. Deep shade outdoors can sometimes have a depressing effect on our emotions, particularly when coupled with moisture. The introduction of light colors through the use of paints, brightly variegated foliage, or cheerfully colored furnishings can liven a dark area.

3. Many other landscape effects can generate strong emotions within us, too. For example, the experience of passing through an enclosed space which suddenly opens up to a magnificent vista or other totally unexpected pleasant sight can be exhilarating.

Keep your analytical eyes open as you observe various landscape scenes and spaces. Take note of the various emotions each scene generates and why it does so. Some of the pleasant psychological effects you experience might prove useful in your own landscape design.

Instant Landscape

A strong force affecting landscape design today is the mobility of our society—the tendency to move on every 5 or 10 years to a new, bigger, and better house higher on the social and economic ladder. This characteristic, coupled with the fact that we all seem to want things right away, has produced within us the desire for immediate effects in landscape design—instant landscape. This desire translates into the planting of large plants (by those who can afford them) or very fast-growing plants.

The biggest problem you'll have to overcome in the planting of large, semi-mature plants is the conflict between your desire for instant green and your desire to spend as little as possible for what you get. Obviously, the older and more mature a plant is, the more expensive it will be. Another factor in the planting of older plants is that they recover much more slowly from the shock of transplanting than younger ones do. It's not unusual, for example, to find a smaller plant catching up to and even exceeding the growth of a larger specimen of the same species in a very few years. Smaller plants have less trauma to overcome before they regain full growth capacity.

Fast-growing plants are usually not all they're cracked up to be either. More often than not, the really fast-growing ones are short-lived, are highly susceptible to insect damage (typically from borers) because of soft, succulent growth, and are structurally weak (brittle, easily broken branches—dangerous in a wind storm). Fast-growing plants certainly have their uses, but usually not as the mainstay of the design.

The solution to this dilemma lies first of all in realizing that many plants commonly thought of as slow-growing (Live Oak, for example) can, with good horticultural care, be coaxed into suprisingly rapid growth. The other part of the solution is careful selection of materials in order to obtain the right plant for the job, in a size that has a reasonable initial effect without breaking the bank—a real balancing act. Add to all of this a little patience, and the solution is complete.

Styles of Design

Should you design a formal or an informal garden? One that is tropical or one that's desert-like? Native? Oriental? Decisions, decisions, decisions.

Let's back up for a moment. In the preceding chapter I mentioned that one of the tenets of current landscape design theory is that the design should emanate from and respond to the nature of the site (including the climatic conditions found at the site). In addition, the previous section of this chapter said that, to be successful, a landscape design must be beautiful, comfortable to be in, convenient to use, easy to maintain, flexible (able to change or be changed), and safe to use. In other words, it must respond not only to basic principles of good design but to the specific criteria you establish in your program.

All well and good, you say, but none of that tells me anything about design style. Correct, and here's why: If you let yourself be tied down by the preconceived ideas of a particular style, you're likely to miss the best solutions to your functional

(text continued on page 34)

Tips for Creating Design Styles

Your garden design needs a theme, a common element (or elements) to make it a unified whole. If you follow the suggestions in this book, you'll probably develop your own design style, which will help you create a unified design.

As an alternative, or in addition, you may want to use as a design resource one of the distinct design styles that have developed through many centuries of landscape design. If you have sufficient design skill, you may be able to combine the features of one style with those of another.

Here, then, are some suggestions to help impart the essence of a particular style to your design. For each style I have listed several major characteristics and components. You can probably add many more. These are presented as a springboard for your own ideas.

General Styles

Formal

Bilateral symmetry, clipped plantings, geometrically-shaped plants (Sweetgum, pyramidal Junipers), orderly rows of plants regularly spaced, traditional garden art (statues for example), central decorative fountain, "crisp" materials (smooth painted wood, cut stone, brick), everything neatly manicured and orderly.

Formal

Informal

Plants allowed to develop their natural forms (unclipped but not untrained), irregular arrangement and spacing of plants and other garden elements (asymmetrical).

Informal (Design by Ross Palmer)

Oriental

Ethnic Styles

Oriental

Sometimes informal, other times a curious combination of formal (clipped individual plants) and informal (irregular arrangements), generous use of stone (smooth river rocks, boulders, stepping stones), naturalistic water features (streams, pools, waterfalls), stone water basins, stone lanterns, arched wooden bridge, boulders arranged in a "sea" of sand or gravel, bamboo fence, dry stream bed suggesting the presence of water, Kurume Azaleas, Bamboo, dwarf conifers, flowering fruit trees, colors mostly green except for fall color, small-scale effects.

Mexican

Courtyards, flowers in decorative terra cotta pots, bright colors (in plants, furniture, wall decorations), heavy wooden shade structures and arbors, irregular field stone pavement, Mexican tile pavement, raised decorative pools of water, stucco walls, either desert-like or tropical plants or a combination of the two, plants in formal or informal arrangements but unclipped in any case, gravel surfacing under some plantings.

Mexican

Desert-like

Ecological Styles

Desert-Like (Dry or Cactus Garden)

Desert, semi-desert (cactus, Yucca), or other plants naturally adapted to a life with little water (Rosemary, Santolina), sand or gravel surfacing, irregular arrangements, occasional boulders, colors generally in the gray-green, olive-green, or silver-green ranges.

This style is not well-suited to southern gardens for two reasons: (1) it is grossly out of character with the nature of most southern climates and vegetation; and (2) the plants necessary to create this style often do not survive the generous amounts of rainfall of most of the South, particularly in those areas with heavy gumbo clay soils.

Tropical

Lush and informal plantings, plants with large leaves (Fatsia, Loquat); informal pools of water surrounded by lush plantings, all ground surfaces covered with groundcovers (manicured lawns destroy the tropical effect), all evergreen plantings, waterfalls, foot bridge across a small stream.

The tropical effect is often difficult to maintain throughout the winter in all but the warmest southern climates, since many of the semi-tropical plants needed for this effect are tender. For more on this subject see *Tropical Gardening Along the Gulf Coast* by Gerald K. Arp (Pacesetter Press/-Gulf Publishing Co., Houston, Texas, 1978).

Tropical

Native

This is a garden style you'll have to develop yourself because it's based on the plant associations natural to your area. For more, see page 75.

(text continued from page 32)

problems. Let your program and site analysis dictate the basic design solution (placement of areas, views, etc.) and then apply the *design characteristics* of a particular style or theme (see the above for some of these techniques). Keep in mind the style of your house and the basic character of the neighborhood (if other than typical mixed suburbia) when selecting a landscape style. The style of your landscape need not match that of your house or neighborhood, but it should at least harmonize.

I emphasize the use of the *design characteristics* of a particular style for a good reason. Any attempt to transplant verbatim the design of another garden into yours is doomed to failure because you're taking it out of context. The other garden design, if truly successful, came about in response to a specific set of design criteria couched within a particular family or social situation. Since your situation is different from any other, your design criteria must be different as well.

Elements of the Garden

Anything complex is most easily understood if it can be broken down into parts that can be studied one at a time. In this chapter I've done just that by dividing the home landscape into what I'm calling the elements of the garden: basics (grading, drainage, and utilities); surfacing; enclosure; shelter; and enrichment.

Think of the garden as an outdoor room. The basics are the foundation of the garden just as your house is built upon a foundation. Garden surfacing equates to the flooring of your house, enclosure to the walls, shelter to the roof, and enrichment to the furnishings. With this in mind, let's begin.

Basics

All landscape design begins with the land as its foundation. Before anything can be constructed or planted, the necessary underground utilities must be installed and the ground itself must be shaped to its final form. These problems of topography and utilities are confronted to some degree on all landscape development projects.

The unfortunate and often discouraging thing about these basics of landscape development is that you can spend a lot of money on them with little apparent progress. This is particularly true of underground utilities. Since you are now aware of this, you can plan your landscape budget accordingly.

Grading

In most residential situations the major grading work has already been done by the builder before you buy the house. You may find it necessary, however, to make modifications to the builder's basic work for these reasons:

1. To improve drainage or change it to fit your landscape development plan (this will be discussed in the next section).

2. To create flat areas for specific uses (paved terrace, games, etc.)

3. For environmental control and for purely esthetic reasons (earth berms or mounds).

Grading is tough work, and unless your grading requirements are very small, you'll find it best to hire a contractor. Machinery and a good operator can accomplish in a few minutes what would take you days to do by hand. Once the contractor has done all he can with his equipment, you can add the finishing touches by hand, smoothing the surface in preparation for planting or paving.

Creating Flat Areas. For the land to be of greatest use to us, it must be essentially level. Terraces, garden buildings, vegetable gardens, lawns for games—all require level land. Some activities can be adapted to sloped areas (see the KIT, page 93), but as slopes become steeper their usefulness decreases to the point where even the soil won't stay in place.

Sometimes the creation of flat areas is necessary in order to provide a stable visual base for your house. For example, the land may slope sharply away from the foundation of your house, making it appear as though it could tumble downhill at any moment. The solution could be a flat terrace between the house and the slope, or perhaps several terraces with no slope at all.

One way to create a flat area without grading is by using a wood deck. Although a wood deck is relatively expensive, it may be a more economical solution than extensive grading and construction of retaining walls.

Grading to create flat areas is done by one of three methods: (1) cutting into the slope in some areas and filling in others (balancing cut and fill), (2) filling only, and (3) cutting only. In any case the final elevation of the level areas is determined partially by the elevation of the ground surrounding

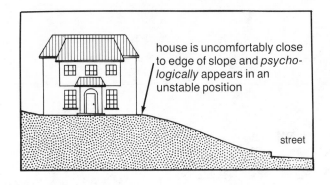

house is uncomfortably close to edge of slope and *psychologically* appears in an unstable position

street

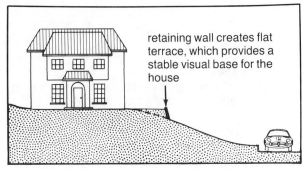

retaining wall creates flat terrace, which provides a stable visual base for the house

Houses situated on sloping land often appear awkward and unstable. Sensitive site grading can help.

your property and of the ground around existing elements such as buildings, trees, rock outcroppings, etc. Grading of the ground around trees requires special attention in order to preserve them. A valuable source of information on this subject is *Trees for Southern Landscapes* by William D. Adams (Pacesetter Press/Gulf Publishing Co., Houston, Tx., 1976).

The creation of level use areas from sloping land automatically generates the need to effect some sort of transition between levels of different elevation. This can be done with retaining walls, steps, paved ramps, or planted slopes. Of course, the more extensive the requirement for grading to create the flat areas, the more expensive the solution will be, both in the cost of grading work and the cost of the necessary means for negotiating the transition (steps, walls, etc.).

Slopes are usually the least expensive solution to the problem of level changes, particularly if the difference in elevation between levels is only a few feet. As the horizontal distance available for the slope decreases, the steepness of the slope will increase until the use of a slope is no longer possible (see the KIT, page 93).

Gentler slopes (up to approximately 33 percent) can be planted with lawn grass. Steeper slopes (up to about 50 percent) which are difficult and hazardous to mow are best planted with groundcovers.

Retaining walls require the least amount of space to effect a change in grade though they're the most expensive solution. But when the difference in elevation between levels is more than a few feet and horizontal space is limited, a retaining wall of some type is the best solution. Low walls (up to about 3 feet) are relatively easy to build yourself, depending on the materials you use. Also, the structural design of low walls is usually not as critical as that required for taller walls, unless the wall must hold up heavy weights above it such as a car or building.

Unless a retaining wall is very low (2 feet or less), it will become an enclosing element because it will block circulation—and view, if tall enough. Thus, retaining walls sometimes act as space dividers. As such, they should be carefully located so as to help rather than hinder the overall spatial design. Even though you can easily see from one level to another, you've created two different spaces if you can't circulate easily between them. If you want free circulation between levels, consider using a broad flight of steps as a dual-purpose retaining wall.

The materials suitable for use in building retaining walls are many: wood (timbers, railroad ties, boards, round posts), stone (many types), concrete, masonry blocks, and brick. The material used is not as visually important when the main outdoor use area is above the wall as it is when the wall can be constantly seen from a major viewpoint. When the appearance of the wall is particularly important, the materials should be selected so as to maintain unity of the overall design. In other words, they should harmonize with the materials of adjacent or nearby buildings, and with surfacing materials, so that the wall does not attract undue attention. Sometimes, however, the wall itself can be the center of interest, although these instances are usually the exception rather than the rule.

There are many important things to know about the detailed design of retaining walls. I suggest you consult a specialty book on this subject.

If circulation is necessary between levels of different elevation, steps or ramps must be used. Steps require much less room than ramps but are more expensive and more difficult to build. In designing steps, remember that outdoor scale is larger than indoor scale. Consequently, the dimensions of the steps, and therefore the area they will occupy, should be larger (see the KIT at the end of the book).

Ramps must be of easy gradient for walking to be comfortable. The KIT gives maximum grades for ramps. As the difference in elevation between

Retaining walls can be interesting to look at as well as functional if they're imaginatively designed. This combination rock garden/retaining wall overflows with a rich variety of plants tucked in among the large boulders.

levels increases, the length of the ramp increases, assuming you maintain the same percent of slope.

If you use a little imagination, you'll quickly discover many ways to create interesting level changes with steps. For example, it's not always necessary to use the standard 4- or 5-foot-wide steps. You can broaden them so that they extend along the entire border between levels, thereby, maintaining a feeling of unity between levels. Or, you could connect the levels with several platforms or terraces sized to fit the scale of the area, each platform being at least one step below the next. If you want privacy between levels, use narrow steps in conjunction with a screening element (fence or hedge).

So far I've been talking about the traditional use of steps—as a circulation connection between levels of different elevation. But steps can also be used for sitting or for displaying potted plants. And, as I've already mentioned, broad steps can function as a retaining wall without looking like one.

The materials used for making steps are the same as those used for retaining walls, and then some. For lightly used steps, grass could serve as the treads, with brick or wood as the risers. This certainly isn't a low-maintenance idea, but it does add some interest to the design.

Abrupt changes in elevation, however slight, are potentially hazardous. If active use areas are adjacent to the top of a retaining wall, you'll need some means for keeping people from inadvertently falling over, such as a rail of some sort. Another solution is to keep people away from the top of the wall with planted areas, pools of water, or groupings of potted plants.

Improperly designed steps and ramps are a worse hazard than retaining walls. Here are some solutions:

1. Use reasonably slip-proof materials, such as brick, roughened concrete, rough timbers, or masonry units.

2. Illuminate step areas for nighttime safety.

3. Don't put single steps, and particularly shallow single steps, in unexpected places (see the drawing on page 30).

Berms for Environmental Control and Esthetics. Although the shaping of earth into berms or mounds is not a new design concept, it's one that has received renewed interest in recent years, even to the point of becoming something of a fad. As with anything that rises rapidly in popularity, there is much lack of understanding of the whys and wherefores of earth berming. Let's clear the air a little.

First of all, there are two main reasons for shaping earth into berms: (1) to block noise, wind, and view (environmental control), and (2) to relieve the monotony of flatness. In most residential situations there isn't enough room to create berms high enough for environmental control by themselves. For example, to be effective in blocking a view or in materially affecting wind or noise on flat land, a berm must be about 6 feet high. If this berm is to be planted with lawn grass, it should have slopes no steeper than 33 percent to allow for easy mowing. A berm of this configuration would require at least 36 feet of ground space from the bottom of slope on one side to the bottom of slope on the other side, and that doesn't include any flat area on top.

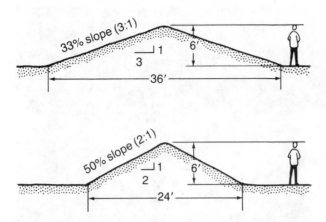

Earth berms high enough to block a view (6 feet minimum) require substantial amounts of ground space. The berms shown here are diagrammatic. If they were shaped correctly (more rounded at the top and bottom), even more ground space would be required.

None but the largest residential properties can accommodate these dimensions and have any usable ground area left. Even a 6-foot berm planted with a groundcover, which can have steeper sides (up to 50 percent), would require 24 feet of ground space.

If you attempt to force soil into berms steeper than about 50 percent in order to conserve ground space, you'll find the results unsatisfactory. You'll have difficulty in establishing and maintaining plants of any kind on slopes of this sort, and in the meantime you'll have problems keeping the soil in place (it will naturally tend to seek a lesser slope). A better solution to environmental control with berms is combining them with fences, hedges, or other plantings placed on top of the berm. Then, neither the berm nor the elements on top need be as tall in order to accomplish the desired effect.

To relieve the monotony of flatness, it isn't necessary to build a berm as high as you might think. Even shallow undulations of the ground (perhaps 1½ or 2 feet high) can provide interesting relief, particularly when combined with planting (a grove of Pine trees at the top of the berm) or with low retaining walls and steps.

One of the keys to successful use of earth berms is maintaining proportions that are in scale with the surroundings. Berms that appear like a bump on the lawn or a pile of dirt that stayed on the lawn so long that the grass covered it cannot be termed successful. In general, you'll be better off if you keep the berm on the low side rather than risk the creation of a monstrosity.

Earth berms fall into two categories according to the way they are designed: architectural and naturalistic. The main characteristic of architec-tural berms is their geometric regularity. This type of berm requires less ground space than a naturalistic berm because it usually has steeper slopes and more abrupt transitions into the surrounding ground. Because of these characteristics, groundcovers are usually the best planting choice. Be sure that the architectural berms you plan to create will harmonize with the area they'll be in and with the character of the remainder of the design. Nothing looks more out of place than a nice, neat pile of dirt in an otherwise natural setting.

A naturalistic berm is one that doesn't look like dirt piled on top of the ground, but like the ground itself gently rising and falling in fluid undulations. On the typical residential lot, such an effect can only be achieved with a low berm, perhaps 1½ to 2 feet at the highest point. The one factor that makes a berm appear natural is a very smooth and extended transition from the berm into the surrounding ground, so smooth, in fact, that there is no evidence of where the berm begins or ends. Consequently, much ground space is needed to create this type of berm.

Perhaps your greatest difficulty in creating a naturalistic berm will be overcoming your desire to really pile up the soil so that you'll have something to show for all that time, effort, and money you spent.

Before you decide whether or not to use earth berms in your landscape development, consider these facts:

1. Plants on earth berms usually require more frequent watering than those on flat ground because the water drains away more quickly. Also complicating the problem is the fact that the south side of a berm dries out faster than the north side (because of the position of the sun in this hemisphere).

2. Earth berms will erode if not covered with something to hold the soil in place and protect it from direct rainfall. The steeper the slope, the worse the problem.

3. Earth berms must be located carefully so as to prevent obstruction of surface drainage.

4. Well-shaped earth berms are created primarily on the ground, not on the drawing board. About the best you can do on your landscape plan is to indicate the general proportions and limits of the berm. The real designing is done with shovel and rake.

The material you need for an earth berm is, of course, soil—but what kind? High berms (from about 3 feet on up) can be made mostly from a decent quality fill soil (no debris) with the top 6 to 12 inches being topsoil. Low berms (up to about 3 feet) are easiest to construct from topsoil alone since there would be only a small requirement for fill soil anyway.

Drainage

In the wet climates of the South, proper drainage is a crucial aspect of landscape development. Chances are, the major drainage pattern for your lot was established by the builder when he originally graded it. However, there may still be problem areas that were never completely drained, or perhaps your proposed landscape development plan requires different drainage solutions.

Your best bet is to work with the existing drainage pattern; in fact, you usually have no other choice. Any major changes will be expensive and could create more problems than they solve, particularly if the changes affect drainage of neighboring properties. If such major changes seem necessary, or if you have severe problems because the property never was drained right in the first place, consult a professional landscape architect or civil engineer.

There are two methods of removing excess water from your property: (1) across the surface of the ground, and (2) through underground drainage systems. The first method is the most common and the one to be used if at all possible.

Surface Drainage. The main goal here is to keep the water moving so that it doesn't puddle, but not so fast that it erodes the soil. This is done by sheet flow across a tilted plane of earth (like most front yards drain to the street), or by chan-

Surface drainage across planting beds need not always be camouflaged. A decorative channel made of short sections of round wood posts, brick, or river gravel will carry water away quickly without erosion. (Design by Bartlett Cocke and Associates, Inc.)

neling the water into a shallow, concave depression (called a swale) and then away from the property (as many backyards are drained—to a swale at the side fence line). Different surface materials require different minimum slopes in order to keep the water flowing. You'll find a listing of these minimum percentages in the KIT at the end of the book.

The nature of your soil can have a significant effect on surface drainage. Sandy soils allow passage of water downward through the soil, a definite plus on flat sites, but on sloping sites they're subject to erosion and must be protected. Clay soils, on the other hand, impede the flow of water downward but are not as erodible. The structure and therefore the drainage of clay soils can be improved by the addition of organic matter, gypsum, or other chemicals specifically made for breaking up clay soils.

Sometimes proper drainage is hampered by improperly located downspouts which pour large volumes of water into an already poorly drained area. Be aware of downspout locations as you plan. Unless you can rebuild the gutter system on your roof, you'll have to work with the downspouts as they exist. If there is no adequate way to remove the water on the surface, consider tying them into an underground drainage system.

Just about any change of grade that you make will alter the existing drainage pattern. If this change can be made so that water can still be removed by surface drainage, you'll be dollars ahead of the game. The alternative—subsurface drainage—is expensive.

Subsurface Drainage. There are essentially three types of subsurface drainage systems: (1) drain pipe with surface inlets, (2) perforated drain tiles, and (3) French drains. The surest and most preferred method is the drain pipe and inlet system. However, this system works only if there is a major storm water drainage system into which you can discharge the water (usually along the street curb). A common solution is to run the drain pipe through the street curb or into the back of a street curb storm inlet or manhole. You must, of course, have enough difference in elevation from the drain inlet location to the discharge point for the water to flow away.

Perforated drain tiles laid underground in a bed of gravel are best suited to sandy soils because the water must percolate through the soil in order to enter the system. There are many books which give suggestions on how to construct this type of system.

A French drain is essentially a trench filled with gravel. The trench acts as a reservoir which rapidly removes the water from the surface and then allows it to percolate into the soil. This method obviously does not work well in heavy clay soils. Even when the trench is sloped so that the water runs into a sump (a large underground hole filled with gravel), it only functions well in clay soils when relatively small quantities of water are involved.

Enclosed or Semi-Enclosed Courtyards. These pose a special drainage problem, particularly in courtyards totally surrounded by walls or the house. Obviously, the best time to provide for drainage of courtyards is prior to or during construction of the house or the enclosing walls. The builder usually does this, but with very small drain inlets and pipe (about 4-inch diameter). This may be adequate if the roof has gutters and the downspouts are tied into the drain line underground. If you have the opportunity to affect the planning of the drainage prior to or during construction, have at least a 6-inch drain line with a 12-inch diameter inlet installed.

If you're stuck with a poorly draining courtyard with a heavy clay soil and no way to add a larger drain line, there may still be a partial solution. You might try a dry well, an 8-inch diameter hole dug down through the clay to a layer of sand or gravel. The hole is then filled with gravel, capped with a short section of pipe, and covered with a grate. Unfortunately, in an enclosed courtyard this will have to be done by hand with a post hole digger, as there is no way for equipment to gain access. You may not be able to dig a hole deep enough to reach a permeable layer, in which case the hole will be only partially effective, depending on how tight the soil is. Three good sources of soil information are your local Soil Conservation Service office, your local county Extension agent, and *The Southern Gardener's Soil Handbook*, by William Peavy, Pacesetter Press/Gulf Publishing Co., Houston, Tx., 1979.

Utilities

Although underground utilities (water, electricity, sanitary sewer, and natural gas) are one of the first items of construction, they are usually one of the last to be designed, and rightly so. Once the landscape has been designed, the necessary locations for underground piping and wiring can be determined. This doesn't mean you need not consider utilities, both existing and proposed, while creating your preliminary and final designs. In fact, if you don't, you may have to revise the design to accommodate some of the utilities you ignored.

Water. In a garden there are many areas where water may need to be supplied, such as proposed swimming pools, decorative fountains, and garden structures (play room, bath house, greenhouse, potting shed). Of course, all planting areas require water applied either with moveable sprinklers and garden hose or through an underground sprinkler system. If you'll be using hoses and sprinklers, you'll need plenty of easily accessible water faucets (called "hose bibbs" in landscape jargon). It's not difficult to add more if you don't have enough or if the ones you have are really in the wrong places. Keep in mind accessibility of the faucets, too. Stepping stones through a planting bed or a slight shift of the location of a proposed shrub can make it easier to get to them.

If you can afford it, an underground sprinkler system can make watering extremely easy and much more effective. The time to design a sprinkler system tailored specifically to your landscape design is after the final plan is complete. Although there are kits and many individual parts available for do-it-yourself systems, this is one area of landscape design best left to the professionals. Professional landscape irrigators, and some professional landscape architects, have the necessary knowledge of hydraulics and of the characteristics of the various types of sprinkler equipment available (See pages 41-42).

One fact to keep in mind is that an underground sprinkler system is much more difficult to install a few years after you've completed your landscape development than it is before that development occurs.

Electricity. There may be a number of items in your landscape design that require electricity, and these must be located in areas accessible to electrical power. Those electrical items that are detached from the house or garage (both ready sources of power) must have the electrical wiring run to them underground, in electrical conduit (pipe). Some of the items that require electricity are garden structures such as a greenhouse, potting shed, storage shed, gazebo, or bath house; garden lighting (free-standing or mounted in trees or on structures); swimming pool equipment; and pumps for decorative fountains.

In most instances electrical work is best done—and frequently can only be legally done—by a licensed electrician. What you can easily do, however, is decide where you need electricity and what appliances must be served (lights, heaters, etc.). The electrician will need very specific information regarding the power requirements of any special appliances you plan on using, such as

(text continued on page 43)

Facts About Underground Sprinkler Systems

Here's one landscape development item that's best left to the professional irrigator or landscape architect. However, in order to discuss sprinkler systems intelligently with the professionals, you should know something about the materials and equipment generally used. There are also a few important design aspects to look for in the plan they will prepare.

Water Meter

The system can be connected to your house meter (usually a ¾-inch size), or you can install a second, larger meter (perhaps a 1-inch size). The larger meter usually requires fewer circuit valves, and if registered with the city water department as a meter for the sprinkler system only, it is not subject to a sewer charge.

Master Shut-Off Valve

This valve, placed on the house side of the water meter, is necessary to shut off the system for servicing.

Vacuum Breaker

An anti-backflow device required by plumbing codes to prevent potentially contaminated water in the sprinkler system from flowing back into the potable (drinking) water system. The vacuum breaker must be mounted higher than the highest sprinkler head. It's best placed in a planting bed or behind a shrub to hide it from view.

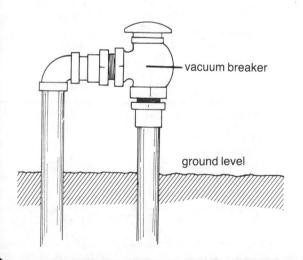

vacuum breaker

ground level

Piping

PVC (polyvinyl chloride) plastic pipe is used almost exclusively. Polyethylene plastic is sometimes used, but it is not as durable as PVC.

Pipe should be buried a sufficient depth to be out of the way of gardening activities. A trench depth of 8 to 10 inches is usually sufficient in areas where the ground doesn't freeze. In colder parts of the South the pipe should be buried below the usual depth to which the soil in your area freezes.

If you have the chance, install pipe across areas of pavement prior to paving. If the pavement exists, don't fret: contractors have ways to push the pipe underneath.

Circuit Valves

These are the valves that turn on each series (circuit) of sprinkler heads. They can be manual valves turned by hand or electric valves operated by a central automatic controller. Hydraulic valves, though not common, are sometimes used.

The number of valves needed depends on the size of your property, your water pressure, and the manner in which the various circuits are to be separated. Here are some logical ways to separate the circuits: grass from groundcovers (different watering requirements), north and east sides of the house from south and west sides (different watering requirements), impact and rotary heads from spray heads (different rates of application), slopes from flat land (require different types of heads), areas under wide house overhangs from open areas (receive different amounts of natural rainfall).

Sprinkler Heads

Lawn Spray Heads. This type is available with nozzles having different areas of coverage (full circle, three-quarter circle, half circle, quarter circle, and special angles), different spray angles (high and low), and different types of spray (fine mist to droplets).

In the pop-up type lawn spray head, the nozzle pops up out of the center of the head when the water is on and retracts flush with the top of the head when turned off. Pop up heights of 1 inch, 2 inches, and 3 inches are the most common, but heights of 6 inches and 12 inches are also made (useful in areas of low-growing groundcovers). Nozzles of the fixed-spray type do not pop up. The advantage of pop-up heads is that they elevate the

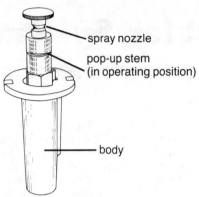

spray nozzle

pop-up stem
(in operating position)

body

Pop-up lawn spray head.

nozzle above the grass blades, thus preventing blockage of the spray. This feature is particularly useful for lawns which tend to build up a lot of thatch.

Lawn spray heads are made of brass, plastic, or a combination of the two. Proper functioning of the heads is more a matter of quality of design and craftsmanship than of material. Cheap sprinkler heads never are a bargain in the long run.

Shrub/Groundcover Spray Heads. In areas of planting other than grass (groundcover or shrub beds, vegetable gardens), spray nozzles are usually mounted on top of a vertical pipe called a riser. The nozzles used are either the same as those on lawn heads or a type made specially for this purpose. Both work equally well. The risers are set at a height that will prevent blockage of the spray by plants. The materials used for risers are rigid plastic (PVC), copper, and galvanized pipe. Copper, which is widely used in some parts of the South, generally looks the best but is more easily bent and broken—a potential problem near play areas and along walkways and driveways.

A special type of fixed sprinkler head for use in planting beds is the bubbler. As its name implies, water gently bubbles out and flows across the ground. These heads, of course, must be located near the ground. Since the water from a bubbler flows across the ground, it can easily flow in the wrong direction if the surface is not graded properly. For this reason, bubblers are best used in very small plant beds or planters.

Pop-Up Rotary and Impact Heads. These heads send out a stream of water rather than a fine spray. They turn by means of gears or the familiar spring-actuated arm which impacts the stream of water and flips the head around. Most are adjustable for part or full circle coverage.

Rotary heads have a nozzle that pops up, whereas the entire head of the impact type pops up out of a brass or plastic container that remains in the ground. These heads are best used in large open lawns because they generally have a much larger radius of coverage than spray heads.

Automatic Controllers

Automatic sprinkler systems use 24-volt electric (or sometimes hydraulic) valves which are turned on and off automatically by an electric controller. Though there are many variations in design and cost of controllers, they all perform the same basic functions—they control the length of time each valve remains open and determine the days of the week on which the valves operate. These controllers are contained in a small metal box which can be mounted indoors on a wall (somewhere in the garage) or on a short pedestal outdoors.

Even an automatic system is not totally automatic. Although there are devices of various sorts which automatically change the method of operation of the controller in response to rainfall or amounts of moisture in the soil, common sense in responding to weather and needs of the plants is still required.

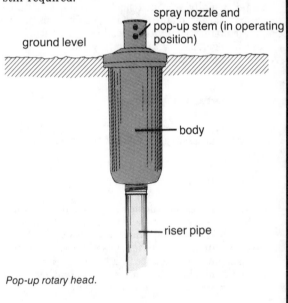

spray nozzle and pop-up stem (in operating position)

ground level

body

riser pipe

Pop-up rotary head.

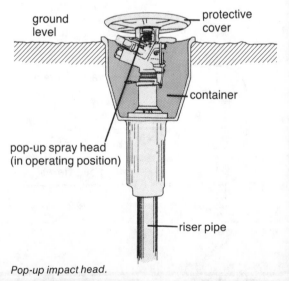

ground level

protective cover

container

pop-up spray head (in operating position)

riser pipe

Pop-up impact head.

greenhouse heaters. You must also decide what type of lighting you want in the various outdoor areas—floodlighting for security and nighttime recreation, soft downlighting from trees for decorative effect, safety lighting for steps, etc. See page 60 for a more complete discussion of garden lighting.

Other Utilities—Sanitary Sewer and Natural Gas. In addition to underground water piping and electrical wiring, you may be planning something that requires a connection to your sanitary sewer system or, perhaps, a natural gas connection (assuming your subdivision has natural gas). Probably the only items requiring connection to the sanitary sewer are a swimming pool bath house and swimming pool backwash (drain) line, and a sink in the garden work center or greenhouse. Both of the pool items would be designed and installed by the swimming pool contractor. You must be aware of them, however, to determine in the design stage whether or not your existing sanitary sewer is accessible from the proposed location of the pool and bath house.

Items that may require natural gas include garden lighting, barbecue grills, greenhouse heaters, and water heaters for a swimming pool or pool bath house. Once again, you must be sure that the natural gas source (a meter) is accessible before planning on including these items.

Surfacing—The Garden Floor

In the preliminary design phase, when you're dividing your site into areas of usage and are determining generally where and what the dividing and enclosing elements will be, you should be thinking in general terms about the flooring of your garden spaces. Surfacing considerations are not always the most important ones, but they certainly are a part of every landscape design project. Although we may not always need fences to enclose us, and the sky might sometimes be the only garden roof desired, every landscape design project has a floor which must be surfaced. Every inch of bare earth (even cultivated ground) must be covered with some kind of surfacing material, because if we don't do it, Mother Nature will.

Functions of the Landscape Surface

The general function of any landscape surfacing is to cover the earth to allow for human use and enjoyment and to prevent the uncontrolled natural processes of erosion and spontaneous vegetative

growth from spoiling our environment. There are, however, several specific functions you should think about when selecting a surfacing material.

A Base for Movement. This is perhaps the most obvious function of commonly used surfacing materials. The surfaces useful for vehicles are relatively limited in number, but there are many different possibilities when it comes to the movement of people.

Different activities *require* (or in some areas are best performed on) different surfacing materials (page 94 of the kit lists the choices of surfacings). On the other hand, the characteristics of a particular material often *control* the type of activity that can be accommodated. For example, the physical texture (roughness or smoothness) of a surfacing material can control the speed of circulation across it and, therefore, the type of circulation that is likely to occur. No one enjoys walking through deep sand or over coarse gravel as a regular habit. Thus, this type of material functions as a barrier to constant movement. Areas surfaced with groundcovers or with water function in a similar way.

Unifying a Design. Many different objects must be put together to create a landscape design. If the objects are not unified in some manner, the result can be chaotic. Surfacing materials, if properly used, can be one of the primary elements contributing to unity of design. Groundcovers function particularly well as a design thread that helps bind together the disparate elements of a landscape such as trees, shrubs, and areas of pavement. When used in this manner, the groundcover imparts a feeling of flowing from one visual accent point to another. In fact, any relatively homogenous surface which encompasses many other elements has the potential of serving as a unifying element. But a landscape surfacing material cannot unify a design by itself. Other aspects of the design must also contribute to its unity.

Transition Between Inside and Outside. The psychological change from indoors to outdoors is often very abrupt, partially because the materials used are different and are used in different ways. Careful selection and placement of surfacing materials can help smooth out this transition. For example, a brick paver used for flooring inside the house and in an adjacent outdoor terrace helps maintain a continuity of experience as you move between the different spaces. This type of transition also contributes to the unification of design of your total home environment.

The size of a paved area also has something to do with the effectiveness of its use as a transitional element, particularly if the surfacing material is different from that used inside the house. A very small paved landing or terrace outside the door does little to soften the abruptness of the transition, so be very generous when sizing these transitional paved areas. But keep in mind the potentially detrimental environmental effects of this pavement on interior spaces (reflected heat, glare, etc.) and make plans to reduce these effects if necessary.

A Base for Displaying Objects. Landscape surfacing, particularly the finer, more even-textured surfaces (lawn grass, concrete, certain groundcovers) can function as a foil or base for the display of other landscape elements. A smooth sheet of water, for example, is a good display surface for a piece of sculpture. A neatly manicured groundcover can be used to set off a particularly handsome specimen shrub placed within it by acting as a simple, stable base which draws no attention away from the object of interest.

In some instances, the "object" on display may be a magnificent distant view. In a situation such as this, the surface in the foreground must be simple in order not to distract from the view.

Pattern. Curiously enough, the sensitive designer can utilize the landscape surface to produce apparently diametrically opposed results in the same design—that is, unity of the design (already discussed) and variety at the same time. One of the major ways of introducing variety with surfacings is the creation of ground patterns, both within a particular material (brick patterns, for example) and by weaving together different materials (groundcovers, lawns, concrete pavement) into a cohesive unit. However, the pattern must not be allowed to draw so much attention that it disrupts the unity of the design.

Types of Surfacings and Their Characteristics

The list of materials useful for landscape surfacing is the broadest of any of the elements of the garden. For clarity and convenience, I have classified them into five types:

1. hard pavement
2. loose and compacted materials
3. lawn grasses
4. groundcovers
5. a special category, water

Understanding the characteristics of each type will aid you in the beginning conceptual phases of the design process. Add to this some specifics about the materials within each type, and you're ready to make some selections.

Hard Pavement

The materials from which hard paved surfaces are made fall into two groups: materials that are poured into place (concrete and asphalt), and materials that are laid as individual units (brick, tile, stone, concrete and masonry paving pads, and wood).

Hard Pavement—Installation. Hard pavement is the most expensive type of surfacing. In general, the installation cost of unit materials (brick, etc.) is higher than for concrete or asphalt, partially because of the higher cost of materials and partially because of the additional labor required to set each unit individually. On the other hand, the unit materials are also the easiest to install yourself, particularly if you set them on sand instead of mortar, which means a significant cost savings over contractor installation. Pre-cast concrete and masonry pads are probably the least expensive hard pavement (also the easiest to install); stone is usually the most costly.

Both concrete and asphalt rank low as do-it-yourself surfacing materials, particularly when large areas are involved. The placing and especially the finishing of concrete require special skills and experience. Wet concrete must be handled rapidly and skillfully or the results will be most unsatisfactory.

Similarly, asphalt requires the proper equipment and skill to create a strong base and to properly compact the surface. But you can handle small areas such as garden paths rather easily.

Hard Pavement—Maintenance. Because of its durability and permanence, hard pavement has the lowest maintenance requirement of any landscape surfacing. Aside from an occasional sweeping or washing, concrete pavement requires essentially no maintenance. Asphalt must be swept more frequently to remove loose gravel that accumulates on the surface, and it occasionally develops holes that must be patched. Weeds, too, can be a problem with asphalt pavement, as they sometimes gain a foothold in cracks and at the edges of the pavement.

More maintenance is required on areas paved with unit materials than with any other hard pavement. Debris catches in joints between the units and on the surface of roughly textured materials. Also, weeds sometimes appear in the joints, particularly sand-filled joints. Occasionally, some of the units may become worn or broken and require replacement. Areas set on a sand base may settle unevenly and require resetting.

Hard Pavement—Environmental Considerations. Hard pavement provides the best surface drainage of all landscape surfacings if it is properly constructed. In addition, hard pavement absorbs and radiates much heat and creates glare, the effects varying with the specific material and color used. For example, asphalt, because of its dark color, absorbs and radiates more heat than the other materials, but it doesn't produce as much glare. This characteristic of heat radiation can be used to advantage if you want to create a winter sun pocket; it can be detrimental to indoor comfort in the summer if an unshaded pavement area is adjacent to the house.

Hard Pavement—Design Considerations. If you need durability underfoot, hard pavement is your best bet. For driveways and parking areas subjected to constant use, your choices are pretty well limited to concrete and asphalt. Few bricks and practically no tiles can withstand such abuse, and any stones that are thick enough are usually too roughly surfaced. If asphalt is your choice, keep in mind that the surface usually is littered with small amounts of loose gravel which is easily tracked into the house. It's a good idea to separate asphalt areas from the house with another surface that will allow the gravel to be dislodged from your shoes.

One use for which the larger unit materials are particularly well suited is the garden path made of individual "stepping stones." These "stones" may actually be heavy stones or they may be concrete or masonry pads or wood discs.

Another unique use for unit materials is as a hard pavement around existing trees. If the units are set on a sand base, they make a pavement that provides solid footing while at the same time allowing air and water to reach the tree roots.

One characteristic already mentioned is that some hard pavements provide a good psychological transition between inside and outside. This is because the man-dominated character of these pavements is harmonious with the same character indoors. Also, because hard pavements are a man-made thing in the natural environment, they almost always are a strong element of any design.

Pavement made of stone is most effective as a design element and as a functional surfacing when the characteristics of the material are fully utilized. Large stone slabs are useful for creating naturalistic pavement that has the feel of solid bedrock. (Design by Robert F. White and Associates)

Just about any surface shape can be created with hard pavement if you select the right material. Concrete and asphalt can be molded to any shape, and irregular stones offer many possibilities as well. The rectilinear unit materials, however, are usually best used in rectilinear shapes; otherwise a lot of cutting is required.

Hard pavements offer a wide variety of surface finishes. The choices range from very smooth quarry tiles and smooth troweled concrete through variously textured bricks and pea gravel concrete to very rough field stone.

Because of the porous nature of hard pavement materials, they are all subject to being stained by automotive oil and fruits. Keep this in mind as you design, since it might affect the location of certain trees that drop juicy fruits or cause you to seek a unique solution for capturing dripping oil.

Of all the landscape surfacing materials, hard pavements offer within themselves the greatest possibilities for creating patterns on the ground. Many interesting patterns can be created through the use of concrete expansion joints, or by using a combination of different concrete surface finishes.

Bricks and tiles are, perhaps, the most useful of the hard pavement materials for creating patterns. There are several basic patterns that have been used for centuries and many additional combinations that can be achieved. The biggest problem you'll have to guard against will be the tendency to become entangled in the creation of interesting surface patterns to the detriment of the other elements of the design.

Special tools and coloring agents can be used to spice up the surface of "plain old concrete" with various patterns and pleasing earth tones. (Photo courtesy of Bomanite Corp.)

A change in direction of a walkway is a logical place to incorporate a contrasting joint material and thus create surface patterns. (Design by author)

One unique advantage that areas paved with unit materials have over concrete and asphalt areas is that they are more easily changed in shape or increased in size. This is particularly true if the unit materials are set on a sand base rather than a mortar base.

In recent years wood decks have become increasingly popular for residential landscapes in the South. They are particularly good for providing a flat, usable surface on sloping sites. On flat sites, decks can be multilevel structures used to provide interesting changes in elevation, or they can be

(text continued on page 48)

Wood pavement in the form of a raised wood deck is an energy-efficient surfacing in potentially hot courtyards surrounded by many large windows. A more heat-absorbing and radiating surface such as concrete would increase the air conditioning load in adjacent rooms during blazing southern summers. (Design by Dick Watt)

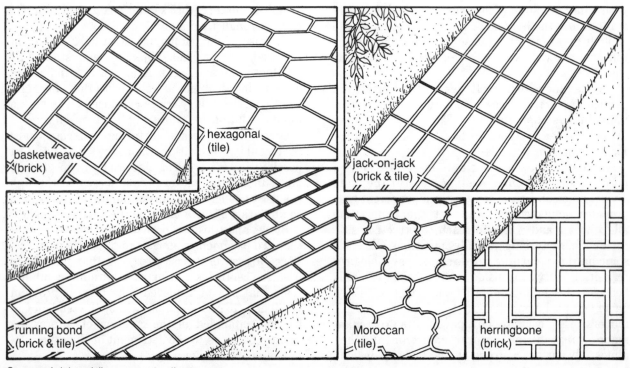

basketweave (brick)

hexagonal (tile)

jack-on-jack (brick & tile)

running bond (brick & tile)

Moroccan (tile)

herringbone (brick)

Common brick and tile pavement patterns.

Concrete Surface Finishes

The surface of wet concrete can be worked in a number of ways to produce different effects. The choice of surface finish should be governed by esthetic design considerations and the appropriateness of the finish to the activity that will occur on it. Here are the choices:

Smooth Troweled

The surface is worked with a smooth, steel trowel which imparts a slick, smooth finish. This finish is useful for floors of garden structures, sports areas, and other places where a completely smooth surface is desired. It's slippery when wet, easy on bare feet, and easy to clean, but it's rather uninteresting in appearance.

Wood Float

A wood float is a trowel made of wood rather than steel. A wood float finish is more porous than smooth troweled concrete and is slightly gritty. Its uses are the same, and then some. As a surface for steps, shallow ramps, and some sports areas, it is better than a smooth troweled finish.

Broomed Finish

Various types of brooms can be used in a number of ways to give the surface of concrete interesting textural and pattern characteristics. The coarser the broom, the coarser the texture. Swirls, checkerboard squares, and a variety of other patterns can be achieved through the dexterous use of the broom. Broomed-finish concrete has several characteristics which differ from troweled concrete. It is more glare-free, and its surface traction is better. The broomed-finish is more difficult to clean and not as good for some games because of its abrasiveness (tough on knees and shoes.).

Exposed Aggregate (Pea Gravel or Pebble Finish)

This is perhaps the most interesting surface finish of concrete. It shows the least amount of concrete of all the finishes but is also the most expensive. The finished appearance of exposed aggregate concrete depends on two factors: the gravel used and the skill of the workman. Colorful gravels, though more expensive than the commoner sorts, greatly enhance the overall effect. However, poor workmanship rather than poor gravel is the most common cause of a low-quality exposed aggregate finish.

Exposed aggregate concrete fits in better with intimate private garden spaces than do the other concrete surface finishes, because its rich color and textural qualities add the interest needed in these smaller spaces. The remaining characteristics of the exposed aggregate finish are the same as those of the broom finishes except that surface traction is not good and it's somewhat hard on bare feet.

Salt Finish

Smooth troweled or wood float finishes can be improved a little in appearance through the use of rock salt at the appropriate stage of curing. Before the concrete is too hard, rock salt is scattered over the surface and pressed in. When the concrete has hardened, the surface is washed to melt the salt, thus leaving a pitted surface. All of the characteristics of this finish are the same as for the smooth trowel and wood float finishes.

Stamped Concrete

For those whose sense of fair play is not offended by one material pretending to be another, concrete can be stamped with a metal tool to simulate brick, tile, and stones of various sorts. The concrete is colored with a dry powder prior to stamping in order to heighten the illusion of real brick, tile, etc. This technique requires skill and experience and should be done only by qualified contractors with the proper tools.

Colored Concrete

There are primarily three methods of coloring concrete pavement. One has been mentioned—exposing the aggregate, the color of which becomes the surface color of the pavement. Another method is painting, and the third is staining. Although relatively permanent paints have been developed which can be used to color the surface of concrete, painting is basically a temporary solution. A more permanent method is the use of dry powders before the concrete hardens or acid stains on existing concrete. Although stains remain longer than paint, some of them tend to fade in bright sun, suggesting that their best use might be in partially or fully shaded areas.

Colors for concrete must be selected carefully to be sure they harmonize with other elements of the design. Generally, you'll be better off with the earth tones (browns and grays) rather than the more obtrusive and strident greens and reds.

simple, single level surfaces used to add the special character of wood to the garden.

The subject of wood decks is treated in several specialized books which you can consult for more details. Suffice it to say that wood decks offer many interesting design possibilities for patios, terraces and walkways.

Loose and Compacted Materials

A second type of landscape surfacing is composed of materials which remain loose and other materials that can be compacted into a semi-hard pavement. Pavements made of these materials have many uses similar to hard pavement, but their characteristics are quite different.

The materials suitable for use in a loose form are gravel, crushed rock, crushed brick, sand, bark, wood chips, and hulls of various sorts (peanut, pecan, etc.). Materials which can be moistened and compacted into a semi-hard mass include iron ore, decomposed granite, blast furnace slag, crushed rock, and soil mixed with lime or dry cement.

Since the characteristics and uses of the materials within each group (loose and compacted) are fairly consistent throughout, they can be discussed as a group. The availability of the individual materials, however, will vary widely throughout the South. There may also be materials other than those mentioned here that are available in your area.

Loose and Compacted Materials—Installation. Of all the landscape materials suitable for use as a circulation surfacing, loose and compacted materials are the least expensive and the easiest for the do-it-yourselfer to install. There are some pitfalls to avoid, however. For example, if laid too thickly, loose materials are difficult to walk on (like walking through dry beach sand). Also, because these materials are loose, they need a confining edge to keep them from mixing with adjacent surfacing materials. Various types of metal, plastic, and board or timber edgers work well, as do concrete and any of the unit paving materials.

Loose and compacted surfaces are subject to invasion by weeds. Therefore, the soil beneath the area to be paved should be sterilized with a herbicide (if no trees or large shrubs are nearby), or covered with a double layer of black plastic.

Loose and Compacted Materials—Maintenance. Debris (leaves, bits of paper, etc.) collects easily on the surface of loose and compacted

The informality of compacted granite surfacing is here reinforced by an irregular edging. An occasional clump of Monkey Grass sneaking into the pavement heightens the effect. (Design by Cornelius Nurseries, Inc.)

materials. It's relatively difficult to remove from loose materials without also removing some of the material, but it is easily removed from compacted surfaces.

When loose material is used as a circulation surfacing, it must be periodically replenished for several reasons. Some is scattered onto adjacent surfaces (a maintenance problem in itself) and some is ground into the soil below, while other material is lost during debris removal. If the loose material is organic (bark, wood chips, hulls), decomposition will claim some of it.

Compacted materials are subject to another problem—they may settle unevenly or the surface may eventually be worn away in spots, thus requiring repair.

Even with proper installation techniques to prevent subsurface weeds, they can still be a problem in the surface layer. So, regular weed removal or herbicide application must be a part of your maintenance program.

Loose and Compacted Materials—Environmental Considerations. Drainage of areas to be surfaced with loose or compacted material must be established prior to installation. Otherwise, loose material will hold water like a shallow pan (if laid on heavy clay soil) and compacted materials will tend to get muddy, particularly if they contain much fine, dust-like material. Conversely, compacted materials can be dusty when dry.

Heat absorption and radiation are greatest with gravel and crushed rock and least with the organic materials (bark, etc.). Glare, however, can be a problem with any of the light-colored materials, loose or compacted.

Loose and Compacted Materials—Design Considerations. Loose and compacted materials are much less durable than hard pavement. Their best uses are for informal, lightly used garden paths and terraces, rustic driveways and parking areas (compacted materials only), and as a decorative non-traffic surfacing (loose materials only). Because these materials are relatively soft underfoot, they are useful in play areas to help cushion falls (loose organic materials particularly). In such situations the material will require replenishing more frequently than usual.

It's possible to create just about any shape with loose and compacted materials. The moldability of the edger used and the requirements of the particular design situation will be the limiting factors.

Areas of loose or compacted material should be separated from indoors by another surface, such as hard pavement or grass, in order to remove loose material which tends to cling to shoes. The effects of dust, mud, and material scattered on adjacent surfaces should also be kept in mind in locating areas surfaced with loose or compacted materials.

Lawns

Lawns are by far the most common residential landscape surfacing of all. Lawns usually are used to cover almost all of the lot not covered by house and garage. This is mostly because lawns are the least expensive surfacing that can provide cover for the ground and a usable surface for people.

Most people already know much of what there is to know about lawns. However, a brief discussion of some of the major factors should help you place the lawn in perspective with other landscape surfacings and, perhaps, point out something you didn't know.

Lawns—Installation. Although there are several grass species and varieties that can be used for lawns in the South, the best choices in each region are usually fairly clear cut. For most of the South, the main choices are St. Augustine, Bermuda, Centipede, Zoysia, and Carpet grass. Not all of these are choices in every region, however. The KIT at the end of the book contains information you'll find useful in helping you select a lawn grass.

While a lawn is the least expensive landscape surfacing to install, the cost is quite variable and depends on two factors: grass variety and method of installation.

If in your area you have several grass varieties from which to choose, you'll quickly find there can be a great difference in cost. Grasses that produce a crop quickly and are therefore more readily available (St. Augustine) are less expensive than the slower-growing, less available kinds (Zoysia). A trip to your local nursery will give you some comparative cost data.

The method you choose to plant your lawn can also greatly affect its cost. The choices are these, in order of highest to lowest cost: solid sodding, plugging (spot sodding), sprigging, and seeding. The KIT contains information about the methods by which the various lawn grasses can be planted.

Lawns—Maintenance. There are a number of factors to consider with regard to lawn maintenance, the main goal being reduction of the lawn's maintenance requirement whenever possible. To begin with, different grass varieties require different amounts of maintenance because of their different growth habits, rates of growth, and cultural requirements. For example, stoloniferous grasses must be edged more frequently than clump types; fast-growing grasses, obviously, must be mown more frequently than slower-growing ones.

Several other factors that affect the amount of maintenance a lawn requires are the shape of the lawn, the nature of any edge treatments, the presence or absence of slopes, and the number and spacing of interruptions in the lawn (plant beds, trees, garden ornaments, etc.). Complex shapes require more time to maintain than simple shapes partially because they have greater amounts of edge to trim and partially because of all the backing and turning required to mow them. Also, the simpler the shape, the easier it is to comprehend visually.

The major time-consuming and back-breaking chore connected with lawn maintenance is edging between grass and other materials. Edging grass against another horizontal surface is generally easier than edging it against a vertical surface, even with the modern maintenance equipment available today. A hard mowing strip or groundcover area between the lawn and the vertical surface can help eliminate this type of edging. Yet, even though one type of edging is being eliminated in this manner, another type is being substituted, admittedly an easier type.

Edgers of any type (concrete, brick, wood) between lawn grass and other horizontal planted surfaces do not eliminate edging as many want to believe (the effect varies with the type of grass). Rather, their primary function is the delineation of the edge of the lawn so that a neater edge can be maintained in the same place every time. But if not placed at the proper level, edgers can create more maintenance problems than they solve. If the edger is placed too low, stoloniferous grasses can easily ramble over it. If placed too high, the problem of maintaining grass against a vertical surface arises. The broader mowing strips also serve as a strong design element, accentuating the shape of the lawn with a strong line at its edge.

The steeper the slope of a lawn, the more difficult it is to mow. When the slope becomes too steep for easy mowing (greater than about 33 percent), the best solution is to use a groundcover instead of grass.

Along with keeping the shape of a lawn relatively simple goes the idea of minimizing the number of objects placed within the lawn. Obviously, the fewer things you have to mow around, the quicker you'll get the job done.

In terms of maintenance cost (both time and money), lawns win (or should I say lose) hands down. In addition to the weekly ritual of mowing and edging must be added frequent watering during hot summers, fertilizing, spraying with insecticides and fungicides, and sometimes replacement of patches that succumb to disease or insects. Groundcovers, though certainly not maintenance-free, offer a lower-maintenance alternative.

Lawns—Environmental Considerations.
Lawns are ideal for helping to produce a pleasant environment both outdoors and, indirectly, indoors. A lawn produces no glare, dust, or radiated heat. Along with hedge and tree enclosures and groundcover areas, lawns help absorb noise and air pollution. They give off free oxygen and moisture (humidity) and thus help freshen and cool the surrounding environment. And, of course, because they totally cover the ground, lawns prevent soil erosion.

Drainage of surface water through a lawn is slow, which is good or bad only in relation to the requirements of a particular situation. For example, on sloping ground, it's important to slow down surface runoff to prevent erosion. On flat ground, however, slow runoff becomes a problem, particularly on heavy clay soils.

The juncture of lawn grass and hard pavement is an area of potential drainage problems. With the buildup of thatch, the lawn can act as a dam and cut off the flow of surface water from paved areas which may have drained properly when first installed. Plan for this possibility by installing drains in appropriate locations or by sloping the pavement in such a way that grass buildup will not stop the flow.

Lawns—Design Considerations.
Because lawn grasses can withstand moderately heavy use, they provide an ideal surface for occasional games as well as normal lounging, light circulation, and an occasional party. But there are several other uses for lawns that you might not have considered.

Normally, lawn grasses are not suitable for driveways or parking areas. Heavy use will deteriorate the grass to the point of being unsightly. However, the combination of lawn grass with any one of several pierced concrete paving materials, which allow the grass to grow in soil pockets, is durable enough for occasional use. Various unit-type pierced paving blocks are available for this purpose. There is also a process called "Grasscrete" wherein special forms are used for poured-in-place concrete. This process leaves holes in the concrete for grass planting.

Because of their relatively fine, even texture, lawns make an excellent foil or background for the display of other plants, art objects, furniture groupings, tree shadow patterns, distant views, and people. Lawns also provide a pleasant contrast with planted areas, producing a smoothing, calming effect, even in small spaces.

Close-cropped lawn grasses, more than any other planted surfacing, reveal the form of the ground plane. This effect can be used to advantage in emphasizing interesting modelings of the ground. On the other hand, slight dips and undulations in what is supposed to be a level plane will also be vividly revealed.

No landscape surfacing is suitable for use in all situations. In the case of lawn grass, there are a number of areas better suited to other surfacings: steep slopes, rocky or very dry soil, wet spots, heavily shaded areas, and areas subjected to heavy daily traffic. In many of these situations a groundcover of some type would be a better choice. In others hard pavement is necessary. For more

How can you soften the effect of a sea of concrete in a parking court? Simple: plant grass in it. The pavement shown here is called "Grasscrete," concrete poured in place with holes left out for grass. (Photo courtesy of Bomanite Corp.)

details on lawn planting and care in the South, refer to *Southern Lawns and Groundcovers* by Richard Duble and James Carroll Kell (Pacesetter Press/Gulf Publishing Co., Houston, Tx., 1977).

Groundcovers

The definition of groundcovers is simple: They are low-growing plants of various types used in mass to cover the ground. But the simplicity of groundcovers ends with this definition. Among their ranks are plants from all parts of the world, representing many different families, genera, and species, and with a fascinating variety of forms, textures, and colors. Plants suitable for use as groundcovers may be shrubs, vines, or perennials (including some grasses).

Groundcovers—Installation. The list of groundcovers suitable for southern gardens is extensive and includes a wide variety of plants. However, the environmental, cultural, and design constraints of your particular situation will considerably narrow your choices. The charts in the KIT should aid you in making a wise choice.

The cost of installing a groundcover bed can vary considerably, depending on several factors: the price of the plants, the quantity of plants required, the amount of soil preparation to be done, and miscellaneous items such as whether or not edgers are used or erosion-control netting is needed (for control of erosion on slopes). Generally, however, groundcover beds cost more to install than an equivalent area of lawn.

Groundcovers—Maintenance. The maintenance requirements of lawns and groundcovers differ greatly. Initially the maintenance of groundcover beds is more time-consuming (watering, weeding, plant replacement), but it tapers off rapidly within a year or two. In the long run, lawns require much more maintenance, both in time and money.

An important aspect of a groundcover maintenance program is selection of the right groundcover in the first place. Many groundcover beds fail to mature properly because the designer attempted to force a plant to grow in a situation that was unnatural to it. There are many groundcovers that can tolerate a wide variety of environmental conditions, but most are fairly specific in their requirements. Your job of caring for them will be easier if you meet those requirements from the start.

Weed control is the biggest problem you'll encounter in maintaining a groundcover bed. The solution is constant attention to pulling or hoeing, mulching, and herbicide application during the initial growth stages. Once the groundcover becomes established and covers the ground (in the first year or two), the weed problems will greatly diminish, though they won't necessarily disappear.

Groundcovers—Environmental Considerations. Like lawns, groundcovers produce little or no glare or radiated heat; they contribute to the reduction of air and noise pollution; and they add free oxygen and moisture to the air. Unlike solid sodded lawns, however, groundcover beds are subject to erosion until the plants cover the bare earth, particularly on slopes, and they're potentially dusty when dry (depending on soil type, mulching practices, etc.).

It's important to know the surface drainage pattern in your yard before locating a groundcover bed so that you don't place the bed in the path of the water flow. If you're not careful, you'll block the flow with a raised bed or cause the bed to be flooded if it's at the same grade as the surrounding soil.

Groundcovers—Design Considerations. Groundcovers are best known as problem solvers. They serve admirably for covering areas where lawns won't grow well, such as in shade, on rocky soil, or in very dry or wet spots. They're also great for seashore conditions, steep unmowable slopes, or small areas between stepping stones.

And the esthetic design values of groundcovers are considerable. They can be used to create patterns of form, color, and visual texture on the garden floor or to help create and divide outdoor spaces. Or, groundcovers can be used as a unifying element to tie together many separate trees, shrubs, and garden ornaments.

In heavy traffic areas groundcovers must give way to other surfacings. Most groundcovers cannot be walked on more than occasionally, and others not at all.

Avoid the common pitfalls of thin rings of groundcover around the base of a tree, or beds that seem to float in a sea of grass with no good reason for being where they are. Neither of these add much to a design; in fact, they often detract by contributing to the chaos of too many things scattered about.

The shape of your groundcover beds should fit the character of the area in which they are placed. This shape is most clearly defined by an edger between the groundcover bed and adjacent planted surfacings. The edger also functions as a maintenance aid, particularly in the case of wide mowing bands.

Water

Water is one material that's not commonly considered in discussions of landscape surfacing. Although water in small basins, raised decorative pools, waterfalls, and sprays cannot be considered a surfacing material, areas of water at ground level such as swimming pools, ponds, streams, and decorative pools do function as a part of the landscape surface.

Water has certain well-known characteristics. But it's the characteristics which the container imparts to water that are of significance to the designer. The container, whether natural or man-made, imparts to water its shape, some of its color, and in some cases its surface texture.

The water container may be rigidly structured in geometric shapes, as is most common in urban landscapes, or it may be completely naturalistic with free edges, as in a pond, stream, or lake. Whatever the container, its shape is important for two reasons. One is that the shape the container gives to the water area is a part of the overall landscape surface design and must fit in with other surface shapes created on dry land. The second is that the surface of water, unless it is moving because of gravity or wind action, is very flat and fine-textured. Because of this simplicity, the shape of the container is emphasized.

The color of water derives from several sources. One is the various minerals held in solution or suspension in the water. Another is the color of the container. The effect that container color has on water color depends primarily on the quantity of minerals in the water and the mobility of the water. The clearer and more placid the water, the greater the effects of container color. Yet another source of water color, in some instances, is the color of the sky. Placid water can be as reflective as a mirror, imitating the colors present in the sky and in surrounding objects as well.

The surface texture of water is a changeable characteristic which depends on the water's mobility or lack thereof. Still water has practically no texture at all, but running water or a water surface affected by wind has varying textural characteristics.

Water has a number of other qualities derived from the form and color of its container as well as from its rate or lack of movement which are relevant to its use as a landscape design element. These are the intangible qualities of quietude,

repose, tension, solidity, exuberance, etc.—all qualities which water in a given container may possess at one time or another.

An area of water can function in many ways in a design. It can serve as a bounding or blocking element and therefore, in a sense, as a spatial organizer because one usually must move around rather than through it. A placid water surface can function as a foil for the display of an art object or a reflection. As a landscape surfacing, water can function to provide these aspects to the garden scene:

1. Coolness—psychologically, and physically through evaporation
2. Sound—bubbling streams, waterfalls
3. Movement—ripples in a pool, streams
4. Mystery—dark water
5. Sparkle—sun glinting on the surface
6. Serenity—reflections on still water

Water areas that are intended to look natural are more convincing if they are placed in a natural position in the landscape—that is, in a hollow or depression as opposed to being raised above the surrounding ground. Also, the design of the water area (its shape, edge design, and waterfalls in connection with it) should be in character with its surroundings. For example, the typical "natural" stone waterfall and stone-lined pool set in the corner of the back yard usually look anything but natural—more like a pile of rocks, actually!

In addition to its endearing qualities, water as a surfacing material has some disadvantages. In some instances, an area of water may present a hazard to small children. Some water areas, particularly placid pools, can provide an ideal habitat for certain annoying or dangerous insects or other creatures. In areas where this may be a problem, proper maintenance can eliminate most of the hazards.

Enclosure—The Garden Walls

In the sense used here, enclosure means any element of a design that serves to confine people or animals to a particular space, either physically, visually, or psychologically. This broad definition allows us to include such landscape elements as areas of water, building walls, retaining walls, planting beds, steep slopes, earth mounds, or a row of pots or trees as well as the typical fences, walls, and hedges.

Three questions you should answer at this point are: (1) Do you definitely need or want enclosure?

(2) If so, how much? and (3) What type is best for the intended purpose? Often, these questions are already answered when you buy the house, by the presence of a fence surrounding the back yard. This practice is standard in some areas of the South and may, in fact, be required by the deed restrictions of your subdivision. The best answers are those that evolve out of the program you have established and your subsequent site and climate analyses. The following sections should give you the information you need to aid you in this decision-making process.

Functions of Enclosure

View Control. One of the major uses of enclosing elements is to control views out of, into, or within a space. Unpleasant views of telephone poles, trash cans, and weedy fields all detract from the garden and must be screened out. Often, merely "breaking up" these views, as with a vine-covered trellis or an open-branched tree, sufficiently eliminates the problem. This design solution works well if air circulation must also be maintained from the direction of the bad view. In other instances a solid enclosure may be the only solution.

Pleasant views can often be enhanced by "framing" them with carefully placed enclosing elements. Many times an enclosing fence or wall can be designed to block out an unpleasant view while at the same time opening up to a pleasant one.

Most of us desire privacy. And enclosing elements can be designed to provide whatever degree of it is needed. Desirable breezes can be retained at the same time with a vertical louver fence; or, short sections of a solid fence could be placed to provide privacy for one area and breezes for another.

On the other hand, we don't want to seem reclusive or unneighborly. It's not always necessary to completely surround the back yard with a fence. Sometimes a partial enclosure, carefully located, will achieve privacy where it's really needed.

The height necessary for the enclosing element to perform its view control function depends on the location of the viewer in relation to the enclosing element. Generally, on flat ground, a 6-foot-high enclosure is necessary to totally block a person's view into or out of a space. Obviously, if the view to be eliminated extends above this height, a taller fence, wall, hedge, tree, or perhaps a combination of these will be needed. In any case, the height should be well above eye level so that the view is totally blocked and not tantalizingly visible just over the top of the enclosure.

The need for view control is not limited to the back yard. If the front of your house is back far enough from the building setback line, as some portions of L-shaped houses are, you may be able to use an enclosing element to create an entry court, thus capturing for private use what would otherwise have been a part of the semi-public front yard.

Sometimes enclosing elements can also be used to block a view from the street into front windows while providing a pleasant close-up view from inside the house. Vine-covered trellises serve well for this function as do strategically located shrub masses.

Control of Movement. Keeping people or animals either in or out of a space, or guiding their movement in a certain direction, is the second major function of enclosing elements. An enclosure need only be dense enough and high enough to control the type of movement desired. A low rail fence, for example, is sufficient to stop the movement of adults (kids love to play on them). A tight-mesh wire fence (chain-link, welded wire mesh) will contain animals just as well as a solid brick wall. Small children and small animals can be contained with a low enclosure approximately 3 feet high. Most often, however, the need to control movement is combined with the desire for visual privacy and the result is a 6-foot-high fence around the yard.

Garden elements that are not usually considered enclosing elements can sometimes function as such. Groundcover beds, a pond, an earth mound, or a steep slope can be used to stop or direct the movement of people.

When you use enclosures to control movement, consider access through the enclosure—a gap or gate. Gates obviously are necessary to contain

The point of access through an enclosure is an important viewpoint into the enclosed space. The entrance itself can be a focal point too—if it's well designed. (Design by George S. Porcher)

children or animals. If the enclosure is being used merely to funnel people to a certain place, a gate is unnecessary.

The point of access through an enclosure should be selected carefully for easy circulation from space to space and to provide good first impressions. Once you pass through a solid, 6-foot-high enclosure, the first scene you see will set the tone for your experience of that space. Keep this important concept in mind throughout the design process. Identify the major points of entry into each landscape space and determine the primary direction of view while entering the space. This will help you determine where to locate features such as specimen trees, sculpture, a fountain, an espaliered tree, etc.

Environmental Control. Noise, sun, and wind are the three environmental factors that can be controlled, at least partially, with enclosures. Noise is difficult to effectively control on a residential scale. In fact, most efforts at sound reduction provide little more than psychological help by removing the source of the sound from view. For more on noise control, see page 28.

Creating shade where and when you want it is not always simple because the sun changes position constantly; usually enclosure and shelter elements must be combined. In general, enclosures provide relief from the sun in early morning and late afternoon, whereas shelters function from mid-morning to mid-afternoon. When both are used together, all-day shading can be produced. For a further discussion, see page 27.

Although shelter can contribute to wind control, enclosures do the bulk of the work. Three wind conditions are involved: (1) strong winds any time of year, (2) cold winds in winter, and (3) cooling summer breezes. The trick is to allow summer breezes to pass through the garden and to eliminate as much undesirable wind as possible.

Research at Texas A&M University into the effects of various enclosures on the reduction of wind speed has produced some useful and often surprising results. For example, it was discovered that pierced brick walls (30 percent open), horizontal board-on-board fences, and vertical slat fences (20 percent open) are better at reducing wind speed over a greater distance than solid or louvered enclosures. (From Robert F. White, "Contemporary Landscape Screens Show Various Effects In Wind Tunnel Breezes," *Texas Engineering Experiment Station News*, March 1958, pp. 8-13.)

However, these test results assumed there were no other landscape elements around to affect wind patterns (trees, other fences, buildings, etc.) Since this is seldom the case, it's important that you analyze the existing wind patterns in your location before deciding which enclosure type you need. It may be that a vertical louver fence will fill the bill nicely.

Most hedges function much like a solid fence or wall, since they are usually thick enough, at least when mature, to effectively block most air flow through them; the wind is pushed up and over or down and under the hedge.

Space Definition and Modification. All types of enclosures define space (set limits to it and give it a shape). A 6-foot-high solid brick wall and a 2-foot-high wooden rail fence can both mark the edge of a space, but they obviously do it differently. There is no standard height or density requirement for this function.

Enclosures are very important in helping to determine the character of a space. This character or mood will be affected by the location of the enclosure in relation to other landscape elements (trees, buildings, etc.) and by the characteristics of the enclosure (its materials, color, texture, size of individual units, height, width, and thickness). The principles of design and the techniques for creating visual effects come into play here (see the preceding chapter).

Types of Enclosures and Their Characteristics

Enclosures can be grouped into two major categories: *structural* and *planted*. Structural enclosures include fences and walls; planted enclosures include shrubs (in the form of hedges) and trees. The following point-by-point comparison should help you decide which you need.

Installation. Fences and walls cost more than planted enclosures, walls being the most expensive. The more unusual the design of the structure, the more it usually costs from a contractor. Hedge cost depends on the size purchased and on the spacing of the shrubs (which determines the quantity). Both factors apply to trees as well. Structural enclosures usually must be kept behind building setback lines and out of easements, and they're sometimes governed as to height and materials by deed restrictions. Hedges and trees are not legally governed by these requirements, though it's wise to keep trees out of easements to prevent possible damage to them in the future should the utility companies need to gain access to their easements for repair work.

Do-It-Yourself Characteristics. Both types require a lot of hard work, but structural enclosures require greater skill and more tools.

Maintenance. Walls require the least maintenance of all enclosures. Wood fences may need to be restained or repainted every few years, and occasionally a board or rail may need to be replaced. Planted enclosures, particularly clipped hedges, require the most maintenance both in time and money (cost of water, fertilizer, insecticides, fungicides).

Immediate Effect. Structures, of course, have an immediate effect and planted enclosures don't. The planting of larger shrubs more closely spaced will shorten the time required to obtain a solid enclosure but greatly increase the installation cost.

Permanence. Properly constructed walls last the longest (longer than you do). The life of wood fences varies depending on the wood used (Redwood, Cypress, Cedar, Pine—in order of greatest permanence) and the care it receives (preservatives, staining or painting, elimination of contact with the ground). With proper selection and care, shrub and tree enclosures will last as long as you'll be in the house. Shrubs that must be constantly clipped or cut back (particularly large-growing ones) eventually become woody and thin and must be replaced.

Design Factors. Structural enclosures offer many design possibilities which are limited only by the designer's imagination and the physical characteristics of the materials available. They require less ground space than planted enclosures. Technical knowledge is needed in designing the supporting structure of walls and heavy fences for safety and to prevent sagging or uneven settling.

Imagination can turn common materials into a uniquely designed fence. (Design by George S. Porcher)

Combining vines and fences can be a tough design problem because the vines frequently grow in the wrong directions. This simple solution has a horizontal design element that doubles as a training device for the vine. (Design by George S. Porcher)

The design possibilities of planted enclosures increase with the amount of ground space available. The arrangement options are these: plants regularly spaced in rows (one or several rows); an irregular shrub mass of one or several species; a mixed mass of shrubs and small trees. Shrubs can be clipped or allowed to develop naturally—shrubs in geometric plantings do not necessarily need clipping. The many different species that are available provide a variety of choices in height, width, and density. Evergreen plants are usually preferable, but many deciduous shrubs offer more color interest if the essential purpose is not to screen winter wind or block a view.

The design of garden enclosures isn't necessarily an either/or proposition—structural or planted. Often a combination can offer some of the most desirable characteristics of each. Even when ground space is limited, structure and planting can be combined if you use vines. They can be used as an addition to a wall or fence for softening or added design interest, or they can be used to produce a hedge effect when trained on a wire fence or light wood trellis. Often vines that grow strongly enough to completely cover a fence or wall will tend to grow to the top of the structure and form a mass there rather than spreading across the face of the structure. Proper training can solve this problem.

Design of a structural enclosure whose axis runs in the same direction as a slope presents a unique and often difficult problem, namely, the need to maintain a stable visual balance between horizontal, vertical, and sloped surfaces. This problem mostly occurs when the enclosure is seen in the same view as a building or other structure with plumb and level surfaces. In such cases a general rule-of-thumb is that the top of the enclosure should be level and stepped down the slope. When not viewed next to a building, the top of the enclosure can slope with the ground.

In any design situation involving enclosures, you must decide whether the enclosure is to be a feature appreciated for its own visual design merits, or a background element. In small spaces there often is no choice—the enclosure will be a strong feature.

Occasionally you may want to highlight a specimen shrub or a spray fountain. The best backdrop for such features is usually a simple fence or wall. A blank house or garage wall can also function very well for this purpose.

Shelter—The Garden Roof

Types of Shelter

Structural. Typically, shelter (a roof over your head) is considered an element of the indoors, and gardens are thought of as being open to the sky. But there need not be so strong a distinction. Contemporary residential architecture often attempts to mesh the two through the use of skylights and loft windows which let in much light and allow a view of tree tops, blue sky, clouds, and passing birds. Another way to produce such an indoor/outdoor feeling is to extend the indoor elements outside, primarily through the use of some type of structural shelter. This solution lacks the air-conditioned comfort of the inside but creates a sense of space that must be experienced for its unique character to be appreciated.

Structural shelters can provide 100 percent cover (gazebos, solid patio covers) or only partial cover (lath structures, vine-covered arbors). They can be either attached to the house or garage (or both), or free-standing. Structural shelters are an important architectural element and should, therefore, be designed to harmonize with the architecture of your house and garage. This does not necessarily mean the style of design must match exactly; rather, the structure should have the same character. All of this is most important when the structural shelter is attached to the house or garage or is seen in the same view. If the structural shelter is a totally separate entity such as a gazebo, harmony of design style is not as important.

The following are several detailed design factors that you must consider. Each is affected strongly by the specific requirements of an individual design situation.

1. *Height of the structure above ground:* This depends on how and where the structure attaches to a building (if it does), the desired feeling of the space underneath (too low creates an uncomfortable hemmed-in feeling), and may be governed by local building codes or deed restrictions. The minimum height required for a comfortable space is about 7½ feet.

2. *Relationship to buildings:* Should the structure be attached to the house or garage? Should it be sloped or flat—and how would this look with the slope of the house or garage roof? You must answer these questions yourself.

3. *Size of the area covered:* In general, your tendency will be to make the structure too small, so think boldly!

4. *Shape:* The nature of structural shelter materials is such that rectilinear shapes are the best possibilities. When the structure is attached to a building, the outline of at least one side and often of two or three sides is predetermined. The shape of free-standing structures away from buildings is, obviously, more flexible. Generally, the outline of the structure should be relatively simple; this allows the observer's attention to be focused on the design of the interior patterns of the structure. Complex shapes and complex roof patterns together can be overwhelming.

5. *Materials:* The traditional and still most commonly used material for structural garden shelters is wood. The supporting structure (post, beams, joists) is almost always made of wood because of its warmth and natural character, which fit most easily into the garden scene. However, in some instances, metal pipes can be effectively used as supporting members, particularly when a very lightweight appearance is desired.

There are several options for the actual roof portion of the structure. Wooden boards, arranged in the form of louvers, slats, or in an open "egg-crate" arrangement, can provide many design possibilities. When solid materials are desired, translucent plastic panels (corrugated or flat), asbestos panels, or canvas can be used. Shade cloth, used in nurseries to shade plant materials, also can provide interesting design solutions.

6. *Relationship to enclosing elements:* Often, it is necessary to combine both enclosure and shelter elements to accomplish the desired function (total sun control, etc.). You'll get the best results if the two are designed as a single unit, having common posts and utilizing the same materials similarly arranged.

7. *Accumulation of debris:* This is a potential problem on solid-roofed structures used in the vicinity of trees. Translucent plastic is particularly unattractive when debris collects on top of it, since

the debris is visible from beneath. You should plan for the means of removing this material.

Trees as Shelter. Trees provide a totally different solution to the need for shelter outdoors. If you prefer the special qualities that only vegetation can provide, there are many tree species from which to choose. The KIT suggests which tree species are useful for southern landscapes.

When trees are mentioned as a shelter element, most people think of shade trees. There is no single set of characteristics that a tree must possess to function as a shade tree. In fact, any tree that provides the right amount of shade at the place and time you want it is, for you, a shade tree. Generally, however, the "typical" shade tree has these characteristics: (1) branches high enough to walk under, and (2) a spreading crown of foliage (as opposed to the extreme verticality of an Italian Cypress). The necessary density of the foliage mass depends on the amount of shade needed.

The following comparison of trees to structural shelters should help clarify your options:

1. *Installation:* Trees are cheaper and easier to install and are not subject to the codes and restrictions that govern structures. Structures must be kept out of utility easements. Though not required, you should do the same with trees. It's also a good idea to keep trees away from overhead utility lines to prevent damage to the lines and severe pruning of the tree by the utility company.

2. *Maintenance:* Generally, trees require more maintenance—trimming, fertilizing, spraying, leaf raking. The requirements vary depending on the species.

3. *Immediate Effect:* The structures have it. How quickly the desired results can be achieved with trees depends on the species selected and the care given them.

4. *Permanence:* A well selected tree will outlast most structures. Quality of maintenance affects longevity of both types of shelter.

5. *Design Factors:* Although there is much variety in tree form, texture, color, etc. within the group of trees useful in the South, structural shelters still offer more design options. Both are strong elements of a design, trees usually winning on this point eventually; so if you use trees, select and locate them carefully to keep them from overpowering the other elements of your design.

If you locate trees for shelter near pavement, be certain they don't have large spreading surface roots that will break up the pavement. The KIT at the back of the book lists some of the worst offenders.

Seasonal variation in the amount of shelter provided is easily achieved with trees through the use of those that are deciduous. Watch out for the leaf raking problem, though.

Vine-Covered Structures. A combination of vines and structures offers a third solution for creating shelter in the garden. The structure required to support vines must be strong and as rot-proof as possible, but it need not be dense, because the foliage of the vine will provide the shelter. In fact, if the structure is too dense (made of closely spaced boards) it's likely to be torn apart by strong vines such as Wisteria.

There are three ways to approach the design of structures for vines. One is to design the structure for the growth habits of a particular vine. This approach utilizes the vine as shelter, with the structure merely for support.

The second approach is to select a vine to fit a particular structure designed to serve a certain function independently of the vine. The vine then becomes an added attraction.

The third approach is to determine the results desired and then design a combination of struc-

Simple arbor-like shelters are ideal supports for vines and cast crisp shadows that enliven surface patterns.

tural shelter and vine that will serve the purpose. Regardless of the approach, you must know the characteristics of the vine before you can intelligently design the supporting structure. The information in the KIT will help you choose.

Vine-covered structures can provide a quicker shelter than trees while retaining some of their advantages. For example, like trees, vines offer the softening effect of foliage and the interest of seasonal change as well as the possibility of periodic color in flower and fruit. Since the structural shelter needed to support a vine can be fairly open, the cost of the structure is reduced.

Functions of Shelter

The major uses of shelters are basically the same as those of enclosures: environmental control, space definition and modification, and view control. Shelters perform these functions, of course, in a different manner. In addition, two functions often performed by surfacing elements can also be accomplished with shelter elements: the creation of a pattern and unification of a design.

Environmental Control. Sun control is the most common use of shelter elements. But the other environmental factors—wind, snow, rain, noise and air pollution—can also be controlled through careful selection of the right kind of shelter.

Most of the important aspects of environmental control were discussed in the preceding chapter. Two other aspects deserve mention here. One is the quality of light allowed by shelter elements. The more diffused light provided by translucent plastic and shade cloth is easiest on the eyes, whereas the striped effect produced by lath can sometimes be very annoying. The dappled light provided by trees and vine-covered structures is probably somewhere in between.

In designing and locating shelter elements, particularly structures, remember to consider air circulation and heat build-up. Solid-roofed shelters trap heat underneath unless they are located in a very open area. If heat build-up is likely to be a problem for you, a more open lath-type shelter or an open-branched tree may be necessary.

Space Definition and Modification. The varying degrees of overhead containment that can be obtained with shelter elements help round out the definition of outdoor spaces begun with enclosure elements. Even the slightest suggestion of shelter—a few beams—can set an upper limit and help create the feeling of being in a separate space though still outdoors.

Very little structure is needed to create the feeling of having a "roof" over your head. Within the same structure, however, the density of overhead containment can be varied to fit the needs of the area beneath. (Design by George S. Porcher)

Shelter elements can greatly affect the quality of a space, the feel or character that it has. By varying the height and density of the shelter, a variety of moods can be created. A grove of high-branching, tall Pine trees creates a space underneath that is very different in feel and size from the space created by a solid-roofed, 7-foot-high patio cover.

Often, the presence of a very open lath structure or lightly-foliaged shade tree modifies the observer's experience of an outdoor space by drawing attention to the sky rather than to itself. In so doing, the shelter has greatly enlarged the sense of space that the observer feels.

View Control. Much of the information relating to view control with enclosures also applies to shelters. In fact, it's frequently necessary to use both for total control. If you need to block the view of a telephone pole or the neighbor's view of you from his second story window, you may need a shelter—perhaps, a well placed tree or patio cover.

Unifying a Design. The use of a structural shelter to physically connect the major buildings in your landscape (house, garage, gazebo, garden work center, greenhouse) is a very effective method of drawing the garden into a unified whole.

The shelter need not be dense to achieve this effect. A very open egg-crate or even a few beams are often sufficient. Once connected in this manner the buildings cease to be separate entities but become a single structure with the spaces beneath the connecting shelter flowing one into another (assuming the other elements of the garden are properly designed).

Structural shelters also help provide a transition between indoors and outdoors by repeating a common indoor element, the ceiling, in outdoor spaces. These shelters provide a softening of the otherwise sharp difference between in and out, particularly when they are attached to the house or when they are near the exits from the house. This is an effect that's difficult to achieve with any other garden element.

Creation of Pattern. Both the shadows cast on the ground or on walls and the patterns of the shelter itself as viewed against the sky can be a significant part of your garden experience. These pattern effects can be very strong and for this reason should be carefully studied in the design stage. Once you've built a lath structure and found that the strong shadow pattern it creates on the

pavement below all but obliterates the fancy join pattern in the pavement itself, it's too late. Create a few mental images as you design and try to visualize the effects of the shelter at different times of day and at different seasons.

These pattern effects are not limited to structures. The shadows of a bare-branched tree against a white wall can be as strong and as interesting as that of the lath structure. It can even be a feature if the wall is the focal point of an important view.

Enrichment—Furnishing the Garden

Basics, surfacing, enclosure, shelter—together these form the framework of any garden design. Each garden element adds another piece to the overall structure of the design and at the same time some enriching colors, forms, and textures. There are additional garden elements that also can provide much in the way of visual enrichment to the garden scene; others are utilitarian and necessary for the functioning of the garden. These elements—such as decorative pools and fountains,

Something as simple as pots artistically arranged on a fence can provide the finishing touch to a landscape space. (Design by Vernon G. Henry and Associates, Inc.)

Shadow patterns cast by lath shelters can be very strong, striping everything under them with contrasting bands of light and dark. You'll have to decide for yourself whether or not such patterns are annoying.

Although difficult to handle effectively, a large collection of enriching elements can produce a very exciting effect. (Design by Michael L. Ilse)

Garden art, such as this bas-relief sand sculpture, has been sadly neglected as a part of contemporary residential gardens. Stained glass, sculpture, mobiles, and many other art forms can be effectively included in your outdoor living areas. (Garden and sculpture designed by George S. Porcher)

outdoor furniture, play equipment, garden art, container plants, rose beds, annual and perennial beds, the mail box, clothes lines, trash cans, storage sheds, and garden lights—could be considered the furnishings of the garden, the accessories. They may be major contributors to the overall design or functioning of the garden; or they may merely be necessary evils.

It's important to keep these elements in proper perspective with the remainder of the design. Without the framework of the design (the other garden elements) there's no place to put the enriching elements. In your home the walls must come before the pictures, the ceilings before the lights, etc. So it is in the garden. Unfortunately, it's not quite as simple and clear-cut as I make it sound. In fact, all of the garden elements, including those intended as enrichment, must be designed together as a unified whole from the very beginning. A decision about one element affects the others as well.

Decorative Pools and Fountains. The characteristics of water in the garden and its use as a surfacing in pools at ground level are discussed on page 52. A few more comments about water features are pertinent here.

Many fountain kits are available with a variety of spray patterns and of varying quality. Often a water basin or other water container is included in the smaller kits. It's very tempting to buy one of these kits, stick it in somewhere near an outdoor plug, and then sit back and watch it do its thing. But the location of decorative pools and fountains, even these small kits, must be as carefully planned as any other garden element. This is particularly true since water usually becomes the focal point of any space that contains it.

Another aspect of decorative pools and fountains is their continuing maintenance requirement. Removing debris, periodic draining and cleaning, and possible servicing or replacement of recirculating pumps are all part and parcel of having water effects in the garden. The larger and more complex the water feature becomes, the greater is this maintenance requirement.

Garden Lighting. You enjoy your garden during the daytime. Why not extend that enjoyment on into the night? Various types of lights can be selected to make the garden safe and secure, to create various decorative effects, to provide nighttime views from the house (by eliminating the normal mirror effect on windows at night), and to make it possible to continue working or playing.

The night-lighted garden takes on a different appearance from its daytime counterpart. The effects created can be very dramatic and must, therefore, be carefully planned, usually in moderation. Your tendency will most likely be to overdo the lighting, to dot lights everywhere or to wash everything with strong light. Duplicating daylight is not the intent of night lighting. In most cases you can create the effect you desire with much less wattage than you might think. Start softly and then build intensity to the desired level.

Garden lighting is more than harsh floodlights on the corner of the house washing a part of the yard with a bright spot of light. In fact, there are three types of lighting effects that are useful in the garden:

1. *General area illumination:* This requires only a low intensity of floodlighting to provide visibility and a connecting link of light between brighter points of interest or activity—you might call it fill-in lighting. Using light in this way helps eliminate the spotty effect you might otherwise have. Also included in this category is the "moonlight" effect, produced by lights shining down from trees through the branches, creating soft shadows and the semblance of moonlight.

2. *Special area illumination:* Included here is the standard floodlighting of game areas; security lighting of house entries; safety lighting of steps or other potentially hazardous areas (particularly important for guests); and lighting of gazebos, terraces, and garden work centers.

3. *Spotlighting or highlighting:* Significant garden features sensitively lighted can provide very dramatic nighttime effects. Specimen trees or shrubs, garden sculpture, and fountains are all suitable subjects.

Your enjoyment of outdoor spaces can be extended into the night through the creative use of lighting. The "moonlight effect" shown here is one method. (Landscape illumination by John Watson)

Striking effects can be created with properly placed lights. One of the most interesting is a backlighted feature such as a large tree. (Landscape illumination by John Watson)

There are two ways to produce this type of lighting. One is to light the background, such as a wall, and thus display the feature in silhouette. The other is to light the feature and let it stand against a dark background. If the feature is near a wall, beautiful shadow patterns can be produced through careful placement of the light source.

Landscape lighting has developed into a profession all its own, yet the creation of pleasant lighting effects isn't beyond the capabilities of the homeowner. One reason for this is the low-voltage lighting system, a system of garden lights which operates at a safe 12 volts instead of the standard 120 volts. This system is usually sold as a kit which includes a transformer, several lights mounted on spikes for easy installation, and some direct ground burial electrical cable. In addition to being safer than standard 120-volt lighting, these lights are less expensive, easy to install yourself (no licensed electrician required), and flexible (easily moved about to just the right location). Unfortunately, the selection of fixture types and design is somewhat limited. This type of lighting system cannot satisfy all your lighting needs, but it can contribute significantly in some instances.

Here are several tips that will help you plan a lighting system for your garden:

1. Endeavor to cast light only where it's needed and keep the source from glaring in the observer's eyes.

2. If you want to spotlight a feature or provide general area illumination, the light source usually should be kept hidden. In this type of lighting, the intent is to create an effect, not to display the light fixture.

3. Remember that, unless concealed, light fixtures become a part of the garden scene in daylight also. They should be attractive and harmonious with other garden elements.

4. Colored lights usually are unsatisfactory outdoors because the colors are too garish and make plant foliage very unattractive.

5. Lights for decorative effect should be on different switches from lights for utilitarian purposes. Chances are there will be times when some will need to be off while others are on.

6. At night the garden is only as large as visibility allows. Lights throughout the garden will show it to its full potential.

Design Ideas for Your Home Landscape

Front yard, back yard, side yard, courtyard—these are usually distinctly separate spaces divided by enclosing elements (fences, walls, hedges, house and garage). Thus, they're best designed as separate entities and will be discussed as such in this chapter.

The design of each separate space must hold together as a complete unit unto itself, and need not necessarily resemble the design of other spaces as long as they cannot be viewed together. In fact, the functions that each space performs and the differences each space possesses will lead naturally to variety of design.

This chapter presents some concepts involved in the design of each of the yard areas and, together with the accompanying photographs, should give you a good start toward developing your own design ideas.

The Front Yard—A Semi-Public Space

To many people, the front yard is just so much wasted space that could be put to better use if some

One function of the front yard is to provide a pleasant setting for the house. Properly selected and arranged plantings and construction elements will meld the house and site together into a harmonious unit. (Design by Dick Watt)

of it were in the back yard. To a certain extent I agree, but not totally. The typical front yard serves two main purposes. First, it is a view space which provides a setting for the house while at the same time contributing to a pleasant neighborhood street scene. Second, it is a usable space which provides access to your lot and house for both vehicles and pedestrians. Although these two functions sound rather simple and straightforward, there are numerous considerations involved in each.

Designing the Front Yard as a View Space

There are three main points from which a front yard is viewed:

1. The primary view is from the street looking across the front yard toward the house. You should be most concerned with the view from the primary direction people will approach the house.

2. A secondary view is from inside the house looking into the front yard through the front windows.

3. Another secondary view, though many times an important one, is from inside the house looking out through the front door. Everyone knows how important first impressions are, but have you thought about leaving a good "last impression"? What do your guests see when they leave your house through the front door? The house across the street? Their car parked at the curb? Wouldn't it be more pleasant to step first into a garden space before entering the realm of the street?

Since most of the elements of the front yard usually are viewed with the house as the background, the visual relationships of these elements to the house are very important. For example, any construction materials used should either be the same as those used in the house or similar enough in character to harmonize.

Colors of the landscape elements must harmonize with each other and with those of the house. Be particularly careful with bold flower colors; ghastly combinations of flower and brick or trim color are all too common. But watch out for the subtle colors also. The slight greenish cast of some pressure-treated timbers can be raucous when viewed against certain house trim colors.

Landscape textures also should harmonize with the house. For example, if your house has wide-board siding, you may need to use similarly coarse textures in plant foliage (large leaves) and construction elements, because very fine textures would tend to heighten the coarseness of the siding by contrast.

Unless you intend to remodel the front of your house, you'll have to work with its features as they are, good or bad. Study your house and decide what you like and don't like about it. Are the overall proportions pleasant, or are they unbalanced in a certain direction? Do you like all of the architectural details?

If you like the design of the front of your house, don't cover it up or destroy its proportions with improperly located masses of plants (shrubs in front of windows, etc.). Instead, use plantings to frame the principal view of the house. This doesn't necessarily mean plop a tall plant at each house corner and let the plantings swoop down to low shrubbery at the front door; it's not that simple. It may mean, for example, that you place a tree so that the observer sees the house under the tree's arching branches. Each situation is unique and must be studied and designed uniquely, not according to preconceived rules arbitrarily applied to all conditions.

If there are features of the house that you don't like, plantings can be used to soften or hide them. Be careful, though, for you might just be drawing attention to the very feature you want to hide.

In attempting to highlight your house with planting, be careful not to separate it from the site with a wall of planting smacked up against it. Pull some of the planting areas away from the house, perhaps all the way out to the street, and begin to create a three-dimensional feel to the front yard. The old concept of "foundation planting" no longer has any meaning and should not be allowed to control the design of your front yard.

In most cases the front door area is the focal point of the front yard, or should be. If your "front" door is on the side of the house, then the gate or other opening to the side yard becomes the front door and attention should be focused upon it.

The concept of unity of design is especially important in the front yard because the entire yard is usually seen in one view, and often a quick one at that. All the various elements of the front yard must be so unified that the overall scene appears simple when viewed from a distance but interestingly varied upon closer examination. This is not always an easy task, for the front yard scene can include many elements: driveways, parking court, front walkway to the house, walkway along the street, steps, retaining wall, earth berms, light fixtures (both on the house and free-standing), house numbers, mail box, decorative entry fountain, screen fence, rail fence, and of course, plants. Although you probably won't have all of these elements in your front yard, you'll certainly have many of them.

The front yard needs enough variety to make it interesting, but it's not the place for collecting or for fussy details. Endlessly complex and seasonally changing perennial borders, circular flower beds dotted about the lawn, rose gardens, cute little bird baths, and other such items usually so divide the viewer's attention that the scene doesn't hold together as a unit. Neither is the front yard the place for tender plants that must be covered with unsightly wrappings in winter. In the South, with the abundance of hardy evergreen plants from which to choose, there's no reason the front yard can't be attractive all year.

Designing the Front Yard as the Entry to Your Home

The front yard is more than just a scene to be viewed; it's also a space to be experienced, primarily while passing through it. Properly designed, it can function as a transitional space between the bustle of the public street scene and your private indoor world. Usually this transition is very abrupt and, for the guest, occurs at the front porch. Ideally, the guest's walk from car to front door should be a time of preparation for the socializing soon to occur. Through selective placement of shrub and groundcover beds, rail fences, trees, or other elements, the entire front yard can become a sort of outdoor entry hall or atrium which by itself says welcome to your guests.

To achieve this effect, you must extract from the larger street scene progressively smaller and more intimate spaces leading to the front door. The intent is not to wall off one space from the next, but to utilize elements that will provide at least a little spatial separation, either physically or psychologically, and still allow a view of the house (groundcover beds, low hedges, a row of open-branched flowering trees, a rail fence, etc.—see the illustration on page 25). In fact, in most instances, building regulations and deed restrictions will not allow any structures above 3 feet to extend beyond the building setback line. The height of plantings,

however, usually is not restricted except at street corners.

Trees are the primary elements useful in reducing the scale of the front yard since they serve to visually limit its upper extent, providing an outdoor roof. A space thus limited can be further differentiated with smaller elements. Front yard trees are also useful in shading portions of the house, and in helping tall houses to appear less top heavy and more pleasantly "tied down" to the site.

Accommodating automobiles in the landscape is always difficult. And aside from the necessary driveway from the street to the garage for your own car, there are additional considerations for guest vehicles. For example, should you provide two or three parking spaces in the front yard adjacent to the driveway, or perhaps a "circular driveway" curving across the yard with two points of entry from the street? Both solutions work for a few cars, but certainly not for the number there will be if you entertain regularly. If you live on a very busy street, you may be forced into providing off-street parking. You'll have to decide for yourself whether or not the expense involved is worth it.

The transition from street to front door can be effectively softened by designing an entry area that comes out to meet you. (Design by Ross Palmer)

This front yard was designed as an outdoor atrium, a smaller, more intimate space within the larger street scene. Upon passing through the entry gate from the street, the guest feels as if he has begun to enter a private world. (Design by Vernon G. Henry and Associates, Inc.)

One of the biggest problems in providing guest parking in your front yard is that, unless you're careful, you may be visually and psychologically extending the street right up to the front door. You can help minimize this effect by using paving materials that differ significantly from those of the street and by breaking up the expanses of pavement into smaller visual units through the use of dividing bands of a different material. Generous amounts of planting that screen out or at least break up the view of portions of the pavement also help. Be careful, however, that the planting doesn't block your sight lines where the driveway meets the street.

A semi-enclosed entry courtyard provides a pleasant, private setting for greeting your guests. Cheerful plantings and interesting enriching elements such as a sculptural boulder or a wall-mounted art piece can begin saying "Hello" even before you do. (Design by George S. Porcher)

Providing off-street parking for yourself and your guests without psychologically extending the street right up to the house can become a major front yard design problem. One solution is the use of a surfacing material significantly different from those associated with the street. Here irregular hard-fired clinker brick is used. (Design by Bartlett Cocke and Associates, Inc.)

Whether you work with the existing sidewalk landing or create a new one, the final design should have a feeling of receptiveness and should be integrated into the total front yard design rather than being a separate entity. (Left—design by Dick Watt; right—design by Ross Palmer)

Regardless of where your guests park, you should provide easy, pleasant access for them from their cars to your front door. Design generously-sized landings both at the car and the front door, and make the walkway wide enough for two people to walk side by side (4 feet minimum). Keep thorny plants away from the walk, but add plants that make the approach to your home pleasant, such as those with aromatic foliage that release a fragrance when brushed against (Rosemary, Santolina, Mint). Place small-scale plants at the front door area to create interesting, intimate surroundings for your guests as they wait to enter your home.

Night lighting is an important and commonly overlooked aspect of your front yard. Creating a yard that says welcome means providing a way to find the right house in the first place (legible, lighted house numbers) and enough light to make entry through the front yard safe and pleasant (lighted steps, a lighted porch, a moonlight glow from tall trees, etc.).

Don't get so wrapped up in your own front yard design that you forget it's part of a larger landscape—the neighborhood street scene. A certain amount of space reduction and separation is necessary within your volume of space, and individualizing your design to fit your particular requirements is valid. But you might consider using the same trees (or at least very similar ones) as your neighbors have if they are good trees and fit other important criteria you've established. This is one way to produce a sense of neighborhood identity and unity.

Think also about what your placement of trees and shrubs will do visually to your neighbor's house. Is it viewed primarily from the same direction as yours? Will your planting block or otherwise destroy the view of his house? Be a good neighbor.

If you have two directions from which the front door can be approached, you have the opportunity to create two distinctly different experiences within the same space. On the left, the guest approach is from the street on a typical front entry walk that was modified slightly to provide a small entry space. The more intimate approach on the right is the owner's everyday access from the driveway. (Design by author)

The Front Yard   65

The Back Yard—Outdoor Living, Recreation, Utility

Unlike the front yard, which is limited in function, the back yard can and usually must accommodate a variety of uses. These can be grouped into three major categories: (1) outdoor living, (2) recreation, and (3) utility. This multiplicity of sometimes conflicting uses often requires that the back yard be divided into several different spaces. However, you may prefer the more open feel of one large space, in which case you'll find it more difficult to design for various functions and still maintain a feeling of unity.

There are several other significant differences between the design of front and back yards:

1. In most instances the back yard is a highly structured space with clearly defined limits set by the house, garage, and fences or walls. It is a more private space. Accordingly, your design can be more individualized, because it need not fit in with the larger street scene, as the front yard should.

2. Ready access between indoors and outdoors and traffic circulation throughout the yard are more important in the back yard, since most daily circulation usually occurs there. Once you've determined the location of the various areas of use, it should be easy to determine the logical circulation routes between spaces (kitchen to trash cans, utility room to drying yard, back door to car, family room door to children's play yard, etc.).

3. Views are an important aspect of back yard design, just as they are in the front yard, but in a different way. In the front yard the primary view is from the street or yard looking toward the house. The primary back yard view is usually from the terrace (or patio) near the house looking out toward the yard. Sometimes there is a very important view from the front entry hall looking through the house into the back yard, and many other viewing angles also occur as the observer moves through the yard from space to space. In short, the view problem is more complex in the back yard.

Outdoor Living

"Outdoor living" means different things to different people. As used here it includes lounging, cooking and eating, reading, sunbathing, and similar activities which usually take place on a terrace, or "patio" as it's called in some parts of the South. Although recreation is often a part of garden activities which include these outdoor living functions, I've chosen to separate it for purposes of

The most useful design is the one that best responds to the owner's lifestyle. This small back yard is designed entirely for lounging and puttering with potted plants. (Design by George S. Porcher)

discussion, and because the spaces required for outdoor recreation are usually separate from the terrace.

Most modern homes are built with some sort of back yard terrace included, usually adjacent to the house. Often this terrace is too small and not in the best location for year-round use or comfort. If outdoor living is important to you and you plan on improving your existing terrace or adding a new one, consider these design suggestions:

1. Make the terrace large enough to accommodate the anticipated activities and furnishings without crowding. It's relatively easy to design a terrace to handle a table and a few chairs, assuming you know the size of the furniture you intend to use. But sizing the terrace for outdoor parties isn't as easy. Before you pave anything, you might try having a "guinea pig" party with the approximate number of guests you normally entertain in order to see if the area you have in mind is large enough.

2. Climate control is very important in outdoor living areas. Proper location of the terrace or patio and the climate-controlling elements (fences, shade structures, trees, etc.) in relation to wind directions and sun angles can increase the amount of time these areas are comfortable for use (see pages 26 and 54 for a discussion of climatic and environmental control).

3. If your existing terrace is poorly located (in a dark, damp corner on the north side of the house, for example), consider adding a new terrace out away from the house in a more suitable location. Terraces located away from the house tend to draw people toward them and thus increase the use of the entire yard. This important concept can be applied equally well to other aspects of garden design: Give the observer something intriguing to

An auxiliary terrace located out in the yard away from the house provides the opportunity for sitting in the garden rather than on the edge of it as with normal back yard terraces adjoining the house. (Design by author)

go to and an easy way to get there and the garden will become a space that is experienced from within rather than just a scene to look at.

4. Easy access to the terrace is important if it is to be used to its maximum. If your current outdoor living area can only be reached by a circuitous or not particularly pleasant route (out the side door and around the back; through the utility room; etc.), consider adding a new one in a better location or, perhaps, adding a new door opening out to the existing terrace.

5. Ideally, a terrace should be a dead end space in the overall back yard circulation pattern. If large portions of the terrace must be kept clear of furnishings so that people can pass through on their way to some other part of the yard, then it's not being used effectively for outdoor living.

6. Often it's desirable to give the terrace a sense of separation or privacy from other garden activity spaces, particularly from children's play yards or very active sports areas. This can be accomplished by using any of a number of enclosure elements of a density that's determined by the desired effect. If you want to maintain view from the terrace but still have it seem set apart, try using a surfacing that's different from the rest of the garden pavement. Or perhaps making the terrace an elevated wood deck would suit you better. Your imagination will generate many good, unique ideas if you let it.

Recreation

Outdoor recreation at home may include any number of activities: basketball, football, baseball, badminton, volleyball, lawn games (croquet, etc.), swimming, general roughhousing, and play centered around various pieces of play equipment.

For many of these activities an open, uncluttered lawn is all that's required (the "open center" concept of back yard design). However, the areas needed for two of these activities—swimming pools and children's play yards—deserve a closer look.

Swimming Pools. Because of their large size in relation to the typical back yard, swimming pools must be carefully designed to be sure they fit into the overall plan rather than disrupt it. One way to do this is to let the needs of the garden shape the pool rather than plugging in some standard shape.

Three very different swimming pools, each designed as an integral part of the overall design. (Designs by: top—George S. Porcher; center—Anthony Pools; bottom—E.B. Flowers)

In other words, design all of the garden shapes, including the pool shape, so that they fit together as in a jigsaw puzzle.

Back yards with swimming pools should be enclosed with some type of barrier fence (not a hedge) in order to control access to the pool—and especially to prevent small children from falling in. Some cities have a swimming pool fencing ordinance that requires a specific type of fencing and self-closing and latching gates.

Children's Play Yard. Play equipment such as swings, slides, and jungle gym sets are often scattered around the back yard lawn. If you have enough space, consider grouping these together into a play area just for children, which will free the main yard for other activities. I'm not suggesting you tuck the kids away in some back corner where their paraphernalia cannot be seen. On the contrary, full visibility of the children's play yard from some vantage point inside the house is important. With a little attention to design, you can make the play area attractive enough to be part of the overall design.

Since the children's play yard usually is not a permanent facility (unless you want it for grandchildren), plan it so that it can be easily transformed into something else that will in turn fit in with the overall design. Perhaps the sand box becomes a pool or a raised planter, or maybe the entire area is turned into a rose garden. If you plan on having only a temporary lull in use of the area, a cut flower or vegetable garden would be more easily re-transformed into a play area for grandchildren.

Pay particular attention to surfacing of the play area. Wheeled toys, of course, need a smooth, hard surface (concrete), but swings, slides and the like should have a soft surface that will cushion falls (grass, bark chips, sand, wood chips, etc.). Any loose surfacing material will require occasional replacement, as it will inevitably be scattered. Grass under play equipment is a maintenance headache and will wear away under heavy use; still, it's good for some situations.

Any plants that might be in or near the children's play yard should be nonpoisonous, thornless, and should not attract bees or other stinging insects. Even stiffly branched plants might cause injury if a branch is broken.

Utility

Trash cans, firewood, compost bins, clothes drying lines, cold frame or hotbed, potting area, soil storage area, boat and trailer parking area, tool and toy storage shed, vegetable garden—these are some of the utility items that must be incorporated into the design of the back yard (or maybe the side yard also). Once again, with a little imaginative thinking, some of these items may not necessarily need to be tucked away behind the garage.

For example, trash can or firewood areas can be screened from view with a vine-covered lattice; the tool shed can be an attractive part of the outdoor living area if a tree is espaliered on its back wall. Vegetable gardens can be arranged in some manner other than in rows and mixed with flowering plants to become a part of the main garden. But be sure you have enough permanent plantings to maintain the design when the vegetables are no longer there.

Since there are so many little individual utility items to be included, it's easy to forget one or two

A children's play house need not be an eyesore. This one was integrated by the owner into an existing landscape. (Design by author and owner)

Utility and outdoor living can coexist when designed to fit together. The greenhouse in this photo was built several years after the surrounding landscape, yet its sensitive design makes it an asset to the space. (Design by author; greenhouse by owner)

of them. The program stage is the time to make a complete list of all these items so that you can plug them into the appropriate places while you're designing rather than tacking them on later.

Remember to plan for easy access to these areas. Garden work center, trash cans, firewood storage area—these and others must be easily reached with at least a wheelbarrow. If you must pass through a gate to reach these areas, make it wide enough to accommodate your wheelbarrow or garden cart.

Side Yards—Nuisance or Asset?

Side yards are really a mixed bag. Front and back yards are usually fairly well defined as such, but side yards often are not. They may be either an extension of the front or back yard depending on where the dividing fence is located, or they may be so separated from everything that they have their own identity. It's these latter spaces that I want to discuss briefly.

These little half-formed spaces between houses, often very narrow and encumbered with air conditioning compressors, gas meters, or electrical panel boxes, are usually just left alone (out of sight, out of mind) or filled up with debris. But since you've paid the same amount of money to buy each square foot of these spaces as you have for the back or front yards, it seems only prudent to pay some attention to their design as well.

Consider some of the uses these side yards can be put to: utilitarian storage (trash cans, firewood, etc.), circulation between front and back yards, and gardens of various sorts (vegetable, cut flowers, roses). You might be surprised how little it takes to make some of these narrow spaces a real

asset. For example, a stepping stone path bordered on the house side with a row of cut flowers is all you need to turn a wasted space into a pleasant experience.

Surfacing is one of the major considerations in very narrow spaces, such as that between the garage and a fence. Grass usually is not appropriate because it is difficult to maintain. If the area must accommodate traffic, use a hard pavement or perhaps one of the loose surfacings. When there is no need to gain access to the area, it can be filled with a groundcover, preferably one that will not create a jungle.

If you have an option, you'll find these narrow side yards more useful when fenced into the back yard rather than left as a back alley of the front yard. Then you'll be able to use them for some of the unsightly functions that shouldn't be seen from the street.

Two different approaches to side yard design are illustrated here. The yard on the right was written off as a loss and left undeveloped. The narrow yard on the left accommodates three functions: circulation, trash can storage (behind the screen), and cut flower gardening (roses). (Design by author and owner)

The Courtyard—Your Private World

The courtyard is a fourth type of residential space which has its own identity separate from front, back, or side yards. Generally, I think of courtyards as small spaces enclosed on all four sides or at least enclosed enough to feel that way. Townhouse and apartment "patios" fit this description, as do many of the outdoor spaces around the newest type of housing—the patio home.

Drainage should be your first concern in the landscape development of a courtyard. If you're lucky, your builder has solved the problem for you. If not, you probably have a very knotty problem on your hands, particularly if the courtyard is totally enclosed. Unless your fertile brain can discover a solution, you'll need professional advice from a landscape architect or civil engineer (see also page 40).

Because most residential courtyards are small, there's a built-in intimacy and smallness of scale to the space. If this feeling is to be preserved, the elements introduced into the courtyard must be of a similarly small scale (small-leaved plants, finely textured construction materials, patterns composed of small units, etc.). Coarseness in such a situation tends to visually diminish the apparent size of the space (see drawings on page 31).

In small courtyards the observer's attention is automatically focused on details because everything is so close at hand. Here is the place for very small plants that are best appreciated on hands and knees; a few flowering bulbs will suffice instead of a mass planting; fragrances can really be appreciated (or be overwhelming). Construction work must be of top quality, for every flaw will be on display.

Furnishings usually play an important role in courtyards—not only tables and chairs but also sculpture, decorative pots filled with annuals, a weathered tree stump, etc. Unity of these elements is as important here as in the larger front and back yards.

The transition from one space to another is often abrupt. In the case of enclosed courtyards, this strong contrast heightens the pleasant, secluded garden atmosphere. As you pass through the iron gate (top photo) you immediately enter the private world of the courtyard (below). (Design by Glenn Cook)

Designing with Plants

Planting design is the unique combination of science, art, and nature working together to produce a living, changing composition with plants. It involves *arranging* plants according to design principles and horticultural requirements (composition), and *selecting* plants to fit your design requirements.

Although planting design is discussed separately in this chapter, it's really a part of the broader landscape planning process. As we continue, you'll see that the planting design steps discussed here fit within the landscape planning steps presented in a previous chapter, "How to Plan Your Landscape."

Keys to Successful Planting Design

Plants are among the least known materials used in creating the home environment. The average person knows little about plant names, plant culture, or individual plant characteristics, not to mention the principles of arranging them into compositions. It's no wonder that many attempts at do-it-yourself landscape design end in failure to produce a really good design. *Plant knowledge,* therefore, is the first key to successful planting design.

But just knowing the facts is not enough. The second key is having the proper *attitude* toward plants. You must learn to appreciate them as something more than objects to be bought and placed here or there. They are living, changing, complex, individual creations in their own right. A little empathy with plants will go a long way toward creating the attitude necessary to effectively use them in plant compositions.

Planting Design Procedure

1. Locate Plant Masses (Composition)

Once you've divided your site into areas of different use and have prepared an area diagram, begin your detailed landscape design by locating major spaces and masses (including plant masses as well as pavement, walls, etc.). Decide where you want trees (for privacy, wind control, etc.) and major planting beds (composed of groundcovers, shrub masses, or perhaps individual shrubs). While you're locating these major plantings, you should also be determining the most important characteristics for each location—height, width, density, texture, form, and color. All of this is done, of course, in response to your previous site and climate analyses and the requirements of your program. The principles of plant composition (discussed later in this chapter) come into play at this point in the design process.

2. Design the Parts of Each Plant Mass (Composition and Selection)

Continue your preliminary design by refining each plant mass into a composition of individual plants or groupings of plants, constantly making sure that all plantings in each landscape space— back yard, side yards, front yard—are fitted into the total plant composition of that space. At this point, you should determine planting area shapes, specific arrangements of plants within each area, and the desired characteristics for each plant. In some instances, a specific plant will come to mind for a particular location. In others, you'll have to be content with determining the desired characteristics now and selecting the specific plants later.

Begin your design refinement with the most important elements of each composition; then, build the remainder of the design around them. For example, the most important element of an entry courtyard might be a specimen plant featured as the focal point. First decide where it should be located and what its characteristics should be. Then design the remainder of the courtyard around it. While locating the feature plant, you must, of course, consider how it will relate to other potential elements of the space.

3. Select the Plants

The next step is to make specific plant selections. In some cases, a single plant will clearly be the best choice—or the only choice. In others, there may be several possibilities. If you can, make several choices for each plant location to maintain flexibility until you make the final selections.

Using the plant charts in the KIT, make a preliminary list for your specific site by eliminating plants that do not fit major conditions or requirements. Keep this list as broad as possible so as not to eliminate any possible choices too soon. Next, take this list to your local nurseries to find out what plants are not available and what others might be added to the list. Then you'll have a final list from which to make your selections.

As you continue to refine your plant selections, you'll need additional information about each plant. Garden books, of course, are a good place to start, but each must be carefully evaluated. Books written specifically for the South are the most reliable although others are useful as long as you understand what part of the country they are written for and can adapt their information to your locale.

Other plant information sources are local botanical gardens and arboreta (if you're lucky enough to have a good one nearby), agricultural Extension service publications written for your area and, of course, local nurserymen and neighbors. Don't expect one source to supply complete information.

Plant Composition

Arranging plants into a composition is an art and must therefore be accomplished in accordance with the principles of design presented earlier. However, plant composition involves more than creating a beautiful landscape. In order for the composition to survive intact for an extended period of time, the plants must be able to tolerate (if not thrive in) the environmental conditions of the site and be physically compatible with each other (no plant overgrowing or crowding out others).

A plant composition cannot be totally successful unless it properly performs the functions required of it by the program, such as sun or wind screening or blocking out a bad view. Otherwise, the composition becomes only fluff around the house—exterior decoration and nothing more.

A plant composition must also be more than a horticultural collection. Although I don't rule out a random collection (or even a methodical, organized collection) of plants as being interesting and pleasant in its own right, it seldom makes a unified composition. Plant collections are usually best located in the back yard in a place where they will not disrupt the unity of a major landscape scene. Perhaps such a collection could become your "secret garden" that you or your guests "discover" as you pass through a screening hedge.

Unity

A group of plants is not a composition unless it visually holds together as a unit—the plants must fit together to make a complete scene. This doesn't mean that all plants must have the same or even similar characteristics. There's ample room for contrast and variety. It does mean that a plant composition must be built around a basic framework of plants with at least some common characteristics (form, texture, color, etc.). Once the framework has been determined, plants of contrasting characteristics can be added for interest. But tread lightly with contrast—it's easily overdone. For example, there's nothing wrong with two very different shrubs being next to each other. However, this same strong contrast repeated in many places throughout the design might be overpowering and disruptive.

The unifying framework of a plant composition must be permanent through all seasons. In the South, with our abundance of evergreen plants, particularly shrubs and groundcovers, this permanency is easily achieved independent of seasonal plants such as annuals, certain perennials, or tender tropicals.

If a plant composition is unified, an observer's eye will move smoothly over the entire composition without severe starts and stops except at focal points. These focal points are prime locations for individual specimen plants of strong character (Crape Myrtle, Yaupon Holly, etc.). As an observer moves through the landscape, he may experience several successive focal points, each best viewed from a particular location. There need not be a specimen quality plant at each location, however. Too many star performers will destroy the design's unity.

Scale/Gradation

An important aspect of plant composition is achieving pleasant scale relationships between the plants in the composition. This primarily means having a gradation of heights from lawns and groundcovers through small perennials or dwarf shrubs to medium and large shrubs, and ending with small and large trees. But there should also be a gradation to some extent in foliage texture, color, and form.

The lower end of the size and texture scale is necessary to bring human scale into a design. The upper end relates the design to the scale of the house and outdoors. In-between elements help tie the extremes together.

Using Color in Composition

Flower color is usually mentioned first in any discussion of plant color. But in plant compositions there are two significant types of color—permanent and seasonal.

Permanent Plant Color. As I mentioned earlier, the unity of a plant composition can only be maintained with permanent elements. This applies to color effects as well. Foliage, bark, and twig colors are all components of a permanent color framework, but foliage color is the most important.

In addition to many shades of green, you'll find that your palette of permanent foliage color includes shades of purple, red, creamy white, silvery white, yellow, and blue. In most instances, a selection of greens should make up the bulk of the color framework with other colors used for contrast. The stronger the color, the more carefully it must be used to keep it from overpowering other elements of the design (thereby creating an imbalance) or clashing with house colors (brick, trim, etc.). This applies to strong greens (dark green, bright yellow-green) as well as more unusual colors.

In a few instances, the color of tree bark contributes strongly to a permanent color framework and can be used to great advantage. For example, trees such as American Planetree (Sycamore) and River Birch have a distinctive bark color (white and tan respectively) that is striking when viewed against a dark background.

Seasonal Plant Color. Flower color is one of the main seasonal variations in plant color, but is by no means the only one or always the most important one. The colorful fruits of some plants (Pyracantha, for example) can be as showy as flowers and often last longer.

Fall foliage coloration of deciduous plants can also be extremely showy, but is short-lived. Winter foliage coloration of evergreen plants, though usually not as spectacular, is a longer-lived color effect and one that may catch you by surprise unless you carefully research each plant's characteristics. A prime example is the winter color change of some Junipers to a reddish-purple or orange-purple. To some people, this is a pleasant effect; to others, the plants look like they're dying. Such a strong effect must be carefully planned.

The same cautions about the relationships of permanent plant colors to house colors apply here. In addition, you must consider the relationships between seasonal and permanent plant colors. For example, will the winter color of Junipers look good with the flowering annuals you had planned to use?

Plant Arrangement Possibilities

There are three ways to arrange plants in a composition: (1) as individuals, (2) as a mass of one plant species, and (3) as a mixed mass of several species. Each has certain reasons for being used.

Plants as Individuals. Examples of plants used as individuals are specimen plants used as a focal point and plants spaced widely enough to maintain their individual identity (whether in rows or irregular groupings).

The main reason for using plants this way is to take advantage of their form (outline and branching structure). Consequently, any necessary pruning should be done in such a way as to heighten or at least maintain the plant's natural form.

Single-Species Plant Mass. A hedge, grove of trees, lawn, groundcover bed, and a vine-covered

Plants with strong forms are displayed best as individual, uncrowded specimens such as this Basketflower clump.

A plant mass composed of a single species is useful for strong delineation of boundaries. Here a row of Pampas Grass also serves to limit view and provide enclosure for a parking court. (Design by owner)

A mixed-species plant mass is useful for creating the variety usually associated with naturalistic and tropical effects. In many parts of the lower South, a mixture of tropical-looking plants combines well with swimming pools to produce the feeling of a lush tropical lagoon.

wall are all examples of single-species plant masses.

Lawns and groundcover beds, by their very nature, are composed of a mass of one species. As such, they provide a simple base within which other plant elements can be arranged. These surfacings are still part of the composition, however, and should be harmonious with the elements placed in them, both visually and functionally.

Plants are often massed together to increase the effect of a particular characteristic (color—massed Azaleas), or to strengthen the effect of a line (hedge). A single-species grouping is also a good way to add strong mass to a composition (to balance another heavy mass elsewhere) while maintaining simplicity.

Often a large mass of foliage can be produced on a wall or fence by using just a single vine. But, some vines grow so weakly that a mass of several plants is needed to strengthen their effect. This is most effective when the same species is used.

Mixed Plant Masses. There are several reasons for combining different species into a mass planting:

1. A mixture adds variety to the design.
2. A naturalistic effect is usually most easily created with mixed plantings.
3. A mixed species plant mass is useful for prolonging the effect of a particular plant characteristic, such as flower color, through several seasons (different species or varieties blooming at different times).
4. A composition can be enriched by a series of different seasonal characteristics coming from the same place in the composition (spring foliage color, flower color, fall foliage color).

In a plant mass composed of more than one species, there should be one dominant species or a dominant characteristic common to several species. Otherwise, the grouping will be too mixed and is likely to appear disorderly. On the other hand, a grouping of species that are very similar in appearance is generally not pleasing to the eye either—much like two paint colors side by side that apparently are supposed to match but that are just different enough to look bad together.

"Foundation Planting" Exposed

Design traditions are difficult to overcome, even when they've lost their reasons for existing. An example is the traditional method of arranging shrubs in a narrow bed that follows the front contours of the house—a method called *foundation planting*. Let me explain why this tradition is no longer valid.

The late 1800s and early 1900s saw the advent of a residential architectural style that resulted in houses sitting high off the ground. In some instances, cellar and basement walls protruded several feet above the ground and formed the visible foundation of the house. Houses without cellars or basements were often built on pilings of various sorts with the floor raised a foot or two above ground. Various means were used to cover the open space beneath the house, one of which was lattice. This open space, the lattice that covered it, or the stone foundations of homes with cellars and basements were usually unattractive and contributed to poor proportions between the too tall house and the lot it sat on. Then, plantings were added to hide

Today's home has no need for the foundation plantings of bygone eras. The designer is now free to arrange front-yard plantings in ways that will tie the house and front yard together rather than separate the two with a leafy, green wall. (Design by Dick Watt)

the foundation and give a more stable appearance to the house—enter "foundation planting."

It was not until the 1950s that the concrete slab-on-grade foundation came into general use. Today, the ugly foundation is gone from most modern homes. Facing materials such as brick, wood, or stucco extend to within a few inches of the ground. Therefore, unless you have a house that sits on a slope thereby exposing some of the concrete foundation, or an older house built up off the ground, you have no need of foundation planting per se— you have nothing to hide.

Arranging Trees

Because trees are such significant elements in the landscape, both in size and effect, their use in plant composition merits a closer look. Here are some points to consider:

1. Trees and utility lines (whether below or above ground) usually don't mix well. Some species of trees are well-known for their habit of clogging sewer lines with roots (Willows for example). Any trees (or other plants, for that matter) planted within utility easements are subject to removal by utility companies needing to repair underground lines, or to severe top pruning by power or telephone companies intent on keeping the trees from damaging overhead lines.

2. While some trees are potentially detrimental to utility lines, others may wreak havoc when placed too close to paved areas. Live Oaks and American Planetrees, for example, will severely crack and lift pavement. (Refer to the KIT for a list of notorious pavement-breaking trees.)

3. In these days of energy consciousness, trees are very useful for modifying conditions inside your house. Place trees on the south or west sides to shade house walls and large areas of pavement in the hottest part of the day. If these trees are deciduous, they will allow winter sun to penetrate and warm the house.

4. In deciding which trees should go where, consider their effect on plantings to be placed beneath them. These plantings will have to endure a progressively worsening condition of shade and root competition, the severity of which depends on the characteristics of the tree. Some plants are able to tolerate these changing conditions, while others eventually need to be replaced with more shade-tolerant species. These new plantings will be a different element in the composition and, therefore, should be included in your original planning.

5. A neat trick for increasing the apparent extent of your tree plantings is to use the same species of tree your neighbors have just across the fence, assuming it's a desirable tree for other aspects of your design.

6. Having trees already on your lot, whether native or planted by a previous owner, is not always a design advantage. In some instances, deciding whether or not to remove a tree is as important a design decision as determining where to plant a new one. Evaluate each existing tree carefully from these viewpoints:

- Is it healthy and good looking (nicely shaped)?
- Does the tree fit into your design? Is it a good enough tree visually to merit creating a special design around it?
- How about its other characteristics? Does it litter, have brittle wood, or destructive roots?

Naturalistic Effects

The creation of naturalistic plant compositions is as misunderstood as planting design in general. The problem usually begins with an attempt to create a little pocket of nature in the midst of an otherwise exotic landscape. A truly natural-looking landscape is difficult to create on the small lots of typical suburbia (though not impossible), but a bit easier on larger properties.

A more realistic goal is the creation of a "naturalistic" composition, one that has the feeling of a natural plant grouping but is obviously not natural. The key is *adaptation* of nature rather than *imitation*, since natural plant compositions are not always visually appealing. Natural group-

What makes a plant composition look natural? When the forms, textures, colors, and arrangements of the plants used are similar to those commonly seen in surrounding natural areas. The undergrowth in this photo is composed of a mixture of native and exotic species almost all of which were planted. (Design by Vernon G. Henry and Associates, Inc.)

ings are primarily functional and are not necessarily arranged according to principles of composition.

Merely using plants native to your area doesn't guarantee that your composition will look natural. In fact, many native southern plants change in appearance under the "fat" conditions of a maintained landscape. Some become bushier; others grow larger and more open than their native counterparts. The plants you use need only look natural—similar in character or general appearance to other plants found growing naturally in your vicinity. For example, one southern plant community contains a shrubby undergrowth of Yaupon Holly, Hawthorn, and several other species with small- to medium-sized leaves and a fairly loose, open-branched structure. In order to create a similar composition, you should use plants with similar characteristics as opposed to dense plants with large leaves (Japanese Viburnum) or those that are commonly known to be exotic (Oleander, Loquat).

In addition to using plants that fit the local definition of "natural looking," you should use them in arrangements and quantities similar to those found in the natural community you are using as a model. Here are some suggestions to help you create naturalistic arrangements:

1. Space the plants irregularly, particularly trees. This means more than just scattering them about in some grouping other than a straight line. It means varying the spacing between plants, even to the extent of clustering several very close together (perhaps in the same planting hole) while placing others off by themselves.

2. A natural plant community is composed of plants in many different stages of growth (different ages). The obvious reason is that they all started growing at different times. When creating a naturalistic plant composition from scratch, you can achieve a similar effect by starting with plants of different ages (i.e., different sizes). For example, a naturalistic grove of Pine trees is more convincing if you plant several small ones (3'-5' tall), some of medium size (8'-9' tall), and one or a few large ones (12'-15' tall). As they grow, they maintain similar size relationships.

The Effects of Time

The element of time plays an important role in planting design. As a plant composition grows older, the processes of plant growth and death work to create a series of slowly changing compositions—an ultimate effect is never reached.

Some of the effects of the passage of time are easily observed while others are more subtle. Here are the major effects:

Change of Size. This is the most obvious change a plant makes. Who would think that a planting designer could ignore this basic fact? Yet, it is commonly disregarded as the overgrowth of many home landscapes demonstrates.

Change of plant size also means a change in the proportional relationships of the composition. These changes will be for the better, if well-planned, because the initial relationships of a young, freshly planted composition seldom are totally pleasing.

Change of Form. Some plants retain basically the same shape and density as they mature—they merely grow larger. Others, however, change drastically. For example, Pine trees generally become less dense; Sweetgum trees change from a pyramidal shape when young to an open-branched, upright shape when older.

Low Maintenance Planting Design Ideas

The ideas presented here suggest ways you can design your landscape to reduce the time required to perform major gardening chores: mowing and edging, trimming and pruning, watering, weeding, insect and disease control, and fertilizing. These are not horticultural techniques but design ideas. Some of these suggestions will conflict with other, more important design criteria, but don't let low maintenance always be the guiding force in your design.

Mowing and Edging

- Keep lawn shapes simple. Design their outline so that your lawnmower will flow freely with a minimum of stopping and turning.
- Use mowing bands or other edgers between grass and groundcover.
- Keep elements such as trees, shrubs, and garden ornaments out of the lawn (put them in groundcover or gravel areas).
- Reduce the amount of lawn by using pavement or groundcover instead.

Trimming and Pruning

- Select plants carefully: use plants that do not develop much dead wood. Do not use plants that are invasive.
- Allow plants to grow into their natural forms—no formal, sheared gardens.
- Space plants according to mature size to prevent crowding and to eliminate the need for constant severe pruning.
- Use fences instead of hedges, perhaps with vines for softening.

Watering

- Install an underground sprinkling system.
- Use less grass and more pavement or drought-tolerant groundcovers.
- Select plants that can survive your normal rainfall with a minimum of extra watering.
- Forget about potted plants, particularly those in small pots. If you must have some, concentrate them in one area for easy watering and use large containers (they'll dry out more slowly).
- Minimize flower beds with soft herbaceous growth that requires lots of water.

Weeding

- Use dense groundcovers to shade out weeds.
- Avoid cultivated beds (vegetable gardens, flower beds).

Insect and Disease Control

- Select plants that have as few problems as possible.
- Don't force plants into growing conditions that are unnatural to them—they'll be weakened and open to insect and disease attack.
- Don't group plants with mutually aggravating problems: Loquat and Pear (Fire Blight), Junipers and Apples (Cedar Apple Rust).

Fertilizing

- Select plants with a low soil fertility requirement.

Change of Conditions. As a plant composition matures, subtle changes in the environmental conditions within the composition take place. Root competition among the plants increases; trees begin to shade out sun loving species below. As a result, plants that are not able to adapt die out—a mini-version of survival of the fittest.

Fortunately for the planting designer, the effects of time on a plant composition are predictable and controllable. The successful designer is the one who anticipates these changes and plans for them. Here are some tips to help you plan:

1. It's important to know what the plants' characteristics will be at various ages and how fast each plant will reach different stages. This will allow you to space them properly to prevent crowding and overgrowth, and to maintain pleasing proportions within the composition throughout its development.

2. If you're the impatient type, you might consider the "planned obsolescence" approach—spacing the plants closer together initially with the intent of removing some of them in a few years before they become too crowded. Or you could include some fast-growing, but short-lived plants for quick green and remove them once the slower growing types have developed sufficiently.

This approach requires ruthless discipline to ensure that removals are made on time. If you soften and keep the plants you planned to remove, your planning efforts will have been wasted and the composition destroyed.

3. Even the most carefully planned compositions cannot be turned over to nature, for the changing design is molded as much by the person maintaining it as the one who has selected and arranged the plants. Pruning (not shearing) is particularly important. It is a horticultural art you should develop early in the game.

What To Do With Existing Plantings

The principles of plant composition discussed in this chapter apply equally to new yards barren of vegetation and to yards with existing plantings, the latter merely having more elements to deal with. If you have existing plantings, here are some suggestions to help you take advantage of them.

Take stock of what you have. Evaluate the health and appearance of each plant, and ignore for the moment, its location. Is the plant pleasantly shaped or has it been grossly misshapen by improper pruning or crowding? Check the larger shrubs to see if they have a good branching structure that could be revealed by pruning (making them tree-like). If you're dealing with an overgrown landscape, you may need to do a little exploratory pruning and removal of weedy plants just to see what you have to work with.

Once you've taken inventory, draw on your base plan those plants that are worth saving. You can decide whether or not they're in the right place once you begin designing. If you have some really nice specimen plants, try to design around them but don't be afraid to eliminate them if they conflict with a major requirement of your program. If they're really worthwhile plants, you might consider relocating them.

Selecting the Right Plant

Because plants are the predominant elements in most residential landscapes (except for houses, of course), your plant selection decisions will be among the most important ones you'll make. And, they will often be difficult choices because each plant must fulfill three requirements:

1. It must be able to tolerate, if not thrive in, the environmental conditions of your lot.
2. It must have the appropriate physical characteristics for its particular location in the plant composition.
3. It must meet other personal criteria you've established (cost, for example).

Because the list of southern landscape plants is extensive and includes a wide variety of plants, you might believe that the choices for your particular situation are almost limitless. But if you do a good job of establishing selection criteria for each plant, you'll find your choices considerably narrowed.

Plant Selection Factors

Environmental and Cultural Requirements. In most instances, you'll find that your plant choices are governed first by what can be grown under your existing environmental conditions, and second by what you would like to grow. Of course, some environmental conditions can be modified by cultural practices (changing soil pH, regular watering to compensate for dryness, etc.) while others, such as temperature, are essentially uncontrollable. Generally, your choices will be better if you respect the existing environmental conditions and select plants accordingly. The environmental factors of soil, moisture, light (or lack of it), temperature extremes, and exposure to wind, salt spray, or other potentially limiting environmental conditions in your area will reduce the choices to a group of plants environmentally suited to your site. From that point, the other selection factors take over to determine your final choices.

In order to select plants for your environmental conditions, you must understand those conditions. To that end, let's explore the major considerations involved in each environmental factor.

There are several things you should know about your *soil* and the *moisture* it contains. You should know the soil's drainage characteristics. In other words, know whether you have a heavy clay soil that holds lots of water, a sandy soil that drains rapidly, or some type in between. Plants ill-suited to heavy soils generally die from suffocation (lack of oxygen supply to the roots) and from fungal diseases promoted by the damp conditions (a severe problem in areas of high humidity). Plants ill-suited to sandy (light) soils generally die from dessication (lack of water).

You should also find out the pH of your soil (whether acid or alkaline) and its nutrient composition (how much nitrogen, phosphorus, potassium, and how many trace elements it has). If you live close to the sea, know whether or not your soil contains salt and if so, how much. Your local agricultural Extension agent can provide information on how to take a soil sample and have it tested by the agricultural Extension service nearest you.

There are two important facts to keep in mind about *light*. The first is so obvious that it's often disregarded: Lighting conditions vary from morning to evening, from season to season, and from one side of the house to another. Light can, of course, be controlled through the use of shade trees, structural shelters, or even well-placed enclosures.

The second important fact about light is: The intensity of sunlight varies from one part of the country to another. This is important to remember when using books to help you select plants. A plant listed in a book written for northern climates as growing in "full sun" might require partial shade in the South, where the intensity of full sunlight is greater. Other factors are also involved, such as the presence or absence of high heat and humidity which may alter a plant's sun tolerance. It is often this complex interaction of light, heat, and high humidity that destroys plants which, according to all printed data, should grow well in the South. Books written for southern gardeners take these factors into account when recommending plants and are, therefore, a more valuable plant selection tool.

For the planting designer, *temperature extremes* are far more significant than temperature averages because it is the extremes and their duration that limit the northern or southern extent of a plant's successful cultivation. For plants commonly grown in northern climates, heat is the major temperature factor limiting or preventing some from being used in the South. This does not necessarily mean that they will not grow here. They will usually grow moderately well for a year or so, then steadily decline in vigor and die.

On the other hand, tropical or semi-tropical plants commonly grown in mild climates such as parts of California, Florida, and southern Texas are limited by the freezing temperatures of winter. Through careful attention to the micro-climatic conditions around your home, you may be able to find a niche for some of these tender plants.

One other significant environmental factor is *exposure to constant wind*. Most plants can survive occasional periods of strong, gusty winds with little or no damage, but many will not thrive under the drying and buffeting effects of constant wind. Plants grown under such conditions are often stunted or dwarfed, a prime example being the typical, wind-pruned plants growing in extreme conditions on windy cliffs above the ocean. Those that cannot adapt merely tolerate the conditions for a while in a weakened condition and finally die. When salt spray is added to the wind, the list of tolerant plants diminishes rapidly.

In selecting plants for a particular composition, it's wise to group together those plants that have similar environmental and cultural requirements. This will make it easier to maintain the various plant groupings and ensure a greater plant survival rate.

Plant Characteristics. Of the many characteristics that plants exhibit, four are of major significance in selecting plants for a composition. You should, of course, consider all of a plant's characteristics when deciding whether it's the right choice, but these four should always be the starting place: *size, form, texture,* and *color* (already discussed).

The mature *size* of a plant is an important fact to know. Whether mature height or spread (width) is the most significant depends on the plant's intended place in the composition. For example, in selecting a plant to be used as a screening hedge, your major concern is finding one that will grow tall enough to block vision. The plant's width is also important in this case because a narrow plant will be more easily and successfully maintained as a hedge than a widely spreading one.

You should also know how quickly a plant reaches its mature size so that you can determine what its continuing proportional relationships will be with the plants around it. Extremely fast-growing plants in a composition of mostly slow-growing ones will soon stick out like a sore thumb unless the effect is carefully planned.

Plant *form* almost always includes the silhouette of the foliage mass and may include the three-dimensional branching structure as well (depending on the plant). Quite a wide array of plant forms is available from low and spreading to very narrowly columnar. Often a plant's form is easily categorized as in the broad umbrella-shaped crown of the Silk Tree (Albizia). However, many plants grow so irregularly as to defy any category except

(text continued on page 81)

Tips on Buying Plants

It's nice to know what you're doing when you buy something. Plants are particularly difficult for the uninitiated to buy wisely because their performance cannot always be determined by just looking at them; and the advice given by young, temporary sales personnel is often less than accurate. Here, then, are a few tips to help you:

Available Sizes

1. Groundcovers and Bedding Plants: flats, pots of various sizes (2½-4 inches), 1-gallon cans. Some groundcovers are also available in 2-gallon cans and balled-and-burlapped. For more information on buying groundcovers see *Southern Lawns and Groundcovers* by Richard Duble and James Carroll Kell (Pacesetter Press/Gulf Publishing Co., Houston, Texas, 1977).

2. Shrubs: 1-, 2-, and 5-gallon cans (a few are grown in 7-gallon cans), balled-and-burlapped.

3. Trees: 5- and 15-gallon cans (sometimes larger can sizes), tubs, wooden boxes, balled-and-burlapped, bare root (only a few southern ornamentals are grown this way today).

The Economics of Plant Size

The larger the container size (or plant size if balled-and-burlapped), the higher the price... usually. But why are some plants more expensive than others in the same container size? There are four reasons:

Here are the sizes in which plants are commonly available (from left to right): front row—flat, six-pack tray, 2¹/2-inch pot, 4-inch pot; middle row—2-gallon can, 1-gallon can, 1-gallon can; back row—5-gallon can, balled-and-burlapped, 7-gallon can. (Photo courtesy of Cornelius Nurseries, Inc.)

1. Newer, patented varieties are more expensive than older varieties whose patents have expired.

2. Plants that are slow-growing or otherwise difficult to grow to a saleable size are more expensive.

3. Less common plants grown in smaller quantities are usually more expensive.

4. Some plants are just overpriced!

Often a smaller plant will outgrow a larger one of the same species or variety in a couple of years because it suffers less transplanting shock. This is particularly true of container-grown plants versus field grown (balled-and-burlapped).

Plant Varieties

1. If you've already carefully selected the plants for your landscape design, don't be influenced by the beautiful blooming plants at the nursery entrance or by "today's plant special."

2. Always investigate unfamiliar plants before buying. Study the plants at a nursery and read about them in your gardening books.

3. Fruit, nut, and vegetable varieties: Find out first which varieties are recommended for your area and which are not (many unsuitable varieties are offered for sale). Local agricultural Extension publications or personnel are reliable sources for this information.

4. Don't be fooled by "look-alikes." In some plant groups (Junipers for example) different species or varieties exhibit very similar characteristics when young, but very different ones when older.

Plant Quality

If you're a novice at plant care, buy only the healthiest nursery stock and leave "bargain counter" plants to the more experienced gardeners who know how to nurse them back to full vigor.

A good-quality plant exhibits these characteristics:

1. It has no insect or disease problems (sometimes these are not obvious).

2. It is well-formed—it has the "normal" proportions and branching structure typical of its species or variety.

3. It has a well-formed root system filling the soil of the container, but is neither pot-bound nor has recently been potted up into its present container from a smaller size.

4. If balled-and-burlapped, it is firm in the earth ball (the trunk cannot be moved back and forth without also moving the earth ball).

upright or spreading. And as we've already seen, the form of some plants changes drastically from youth to maturity.

Your plant compositions will generally be more successful if you allow the plants to develop their natural form. Even highly manicured and heavily clipped landscapes are better when plant forms are carefully selected and arranged—it's easier to keep a plant clipped low and broad if that's its natural form.

Size and form must sometimes be jointly considered when selecting a plant. For example, if you are selecting a plant because of its particularly appealing form, its mature size must not be greater than the space available. If it is, the effect of the natural form will be destroyed.

The third major plant characteristic is *texture*— the overall coarseness or fineness of the foliage mass. This visual texture is composed of many individual plant characteristics such as leaf size, leaf shape, and method of attachment to the plant. Leaf size is usually the most important.

Unfortunately, most books do not mention a plant's textural appearance. Therefore, you must usually determine this by direct observation. When categorizing a plant's texture, remember that it's a relative quality. Whether a plant is considered coarsely or finely textured depends, to a degree, on what other textures are seen with it.

The planting designer's palette of foliage textures is rich indeed.

Landscape Planning and Design Kit

This KIT has been designed as a reference to assist you through the various steps of the landscape planning process. To this end, the information here is, for the most part, arranged in the same sequential order as the text, with the first item being a checklist outlining each of the steps. Only the plant charts are out of order, being located next to the index for purposes of quick cross-referencing of plant names.

Landscape Planning Procedure Checklist

Here are all the steps you should follow in the development of your home landscape. They are sequential and thus are best accomplished in the order given. For a complete discussion of each item see the chapter on "How to Plan Your Landscape" and additional portions of this KIT.*

I. Prepare a Program
1. Family facts
2. Wants and needs
3. Capabilities and limitations

II. Analyze Your Site and Climate
1. Gather pertinent drawings
2. Measure your yard
3. Conduct site analysis and take notes
4. Collect climatic data

III. Prepare a Preliminary Plan and Cost Estimate
1. Gather drawing materials
2. Draw a base plan
3. Review collected data
4. Prepare a site analysis diagram
5. Prepare an area diagram
6. Begin sketching ideas (detailed design)
7. Consolidate ideas into a conceptual plan
8. Refine conceptual plan into a preliminary plan
9. Make a preliminary cost estimate
10. Review and modify preliminary plan

IV. Draw the Final Plan
1. Draw the plan
2. Prepare a bill of materials

---

*As mentioned in the text, installation and maintenance are also part of the landscape planning process although they're not included in this checklist.

Preparing a Program—
A Grab Bag of Possibilities

Listed below are many of the items and considerations that may be involved in your landscape development. Check those that pertain to you and add any others you can think of.

Family Facts

Possessions: Which of these must you accommodate in the landscape?

- ☐ Pets
- ☐ Recreational vehicles
- ☐ Boat and trailer
- ☐ Motorcycle
- ☐ Garden furniture
- ☐ Potted plants
- ☐ Bird bath
- ☐ Garden sculpture
- ☐ Mail box
- ☐ Trash cans
- ☐ Children's play equipment (swing, slide, fort)
- ☐ Barbecue grill

Lifestyle: Are these a part of your way of life?

- ☐ Family or individual hobbies
- ☐ Lawn games (croquet, badminton, volleyball)
- ☐ Outdoor eating
- ☐ Outdoor lounging
- ☐ Outdoor entertaining
- ☐ Gardening for fun
- ☐ Allergies
- ☐ Neighborly relations (inviting them over for recreation, dining, a friendly talk)

Wants and Needs

- ☐ Outdoor cooking area
- ☐ Outdoor eating area
- ☐ Private lounging area (sunbathing, reading)
- ☐ Children's play area (play equipment, sand box, fort, tricycle path, play house)
- ☐ Open lawn for games/entertaining
- ☐ All-weather circulation throughout the yard
- ☐ All-weather sitting area
- ☐ Gazebo

- ☐ Easy access to front door from driveway
- ☐ Off-street guest parking
- ☐ Parking for extra vehicles (boat and trailer, recreational vehicles, extra cars)
- ☐ Entry courtyard
- ☐ Swimming pool
- ☐ Wading pool
- ☐ Decorative pool and/or fountain
- ☐ Privacy from neighbors
- ☐ House numbers
- ☐ Attractive mailbox
- ☐ Garden lighting (decoration, security, night games)
- ☐ Shade (structural shelter, trees)
- ☐ Perimeter fencing
- ☐ Clothes lines (permanent or collapsible)
- ☐ Trash can storage
- ☐ Tool shed
- ☐ Potting bench
- ☐ Compost pile
- ☐ Greenhouse
- ☐ Cold frame
- ☐ Hotbed
- ☐ Bulk materials storage (topsoil, mulch, sand)
- ☐ Dog run
- ☐ Raised wood deck
- ☐ Irrigation system
- ☐ More water faucets
- ☐ Fruit trees
- ☐ Vegetable garden
- ☐ Herb garden
- ☐ Rose garden
- ☐ Rock garden
- ☐ Potted plants
- ☐ Hanging baskets
- ☐ Flower beds
- ☐ Bird feeder or bird house
- ☐ Low maintenance plantings

Capabilities and Limitations

Construction Know-How

- ☐ Carpentry
- ☐ Masonry
- ☐ Electrical
- ☐ Plumbing
- ☐ Concrete work

Horticultural Know-How

☐ Planting methods

☐ Artful pruning

☐ Fertilizing (what and how much to use)

☐ Spraying (insecticides, fungicides, herbicides)

Budget

How much money available initially?
What total amount can you afford?

Time

How much is available daily or on weekends for planning, installation, maintenance?

Site and Climate Analysis—What to Look For

Site

Topography and Drainage

- Flat land may have drainage problems—look for standing water after a rain.
- Sloping land—you may need some grading work to create level areas; look for potential erosion areas; observe drainage patterns from your lot toward the neighbor's and vice versa.
- Rock outcroppings or ledges—these can be used to advantage as a design element.
- Apparently flat land may slope more than you realize. Determine the amount of slope—you may be able to accentuate it and create interesting elevation changes.
- Note the existing drainage flow—chances are you'll have to work with it.

Soil

- Have your soil tested for pH, nutrient levels, other chemical constituents.
- Digging a test hole will tell you about soil structure—tight clay, loose and sandy, or something in between.

Existing Vegetation

- Note the quality of existing trees, shrubs, or vines—health, shape, overall appearance.
- Except for obvious location problems, the desirability of location can be determined during the design phases.
- Learn about the main good or bad qualities of the existing plants—profuse-flowering, weak wood, etc.

House Features (Inside and Outside)

- Points of entry and exit, how frequently each will be used, and by whom.

- Good and bad views from inside looking out.
- Note which rooms are hottest because of outside influences (adjacent reflective pavement, sun angles, etc.)
- Looking at your house, note blank walls, good and bad architectural proportions, the feeling of how the house sits on the lot (stable? teetering on the edge of a slope?). Observe from many angles, noting which are the major views.
- Presence or absence of roof gutters.
- Note the natural light characteristic of each room—is it good or bad for that room?
- Differences in elevation between inside and outside—take advantage of them with wood decks.

Circulation

- Daily access to and from your lot.
- Daily circulation between inside and outside.
- What are the circulation needs around the site (to water faucets, trash cans, clothes lines, etc.)?
- Note relationships between inside areas and potential outdoor areas (den to play yard, kitchen to utility area, etc.).
- Guest access and parking—good or bad?

Views

- Good and bad views from various portions of the site.
- What do others see—from a neighboring two-story house? From the street?
- What do guests see as they approach the house—is it good or bad?
- Can good views be created by removing vegetation?

Miscellaneous

- Flooding—are any portions of your lot subject to flooding from street overflow, adjacent creeks or bayous?

- Do car headlights shine into any rooms? What about street lights? Tennis court lights?
- Any noise problems from nearby streets or busy intersections? How about noise from nearby businesses?

Climate

Temperature

- Extremes of hot and cold (buy a recording thermometer).
- Note pockets of heat where wind doesn't circulate.
- Are you at the bottom of a hill where cold air will settle?

Sunlight

- Observe sun angles at different times of the day and year in relation to house windows, various areas of the yard.

- Where do you have shade? Where do you need shade?
- Reflected light (glare) from pavement.

Rainfall

- How much and at what times of year? (This affects maintenance and plant selection.)

Humidity

- How much and what times of year is it highest or lowest? (This affects maintenance and plant selection.)
- Many existing trees? These will increase local humidity.

Wind

- Prevailing breezes at different times of year (cooling summer breezes, cold northwest winds).
- Seasons and directions of strongest winds.
- Note windy and protected site areas.

Drawings You Should Obtain

Deed Plat (also called Title Survey)

This is a small drawing (usually 8½ x 14 inches) which is prepared by a registered public surveyor as a part of your deed records. It shows the dimensions of your property lines, locates the house with respect to the property lines, shows the basic dimensions of the outside house walls, locates driveways and walkways, and shows building setback lines and easements. With all due respect to registered public surveyors in general, I have found many deed plats to be inaccurate, mostly with respect to location of the house on the lot. It's a good idea to check the dimensions yourself. In the process, you'll become better acquainted with your property and house and probably learn a few things about them that you didn't know.

Architectural Drawings

These are usually available from the builder of your house if it is relatively new. The drawings you'll need are the floor plan of the house and the site plan (showing the property lines, easements, house, driveway, walks, and sometimes the underground utility locations). The elevation drawings

(views of the front, back and sides of the house) might also be useful while you're sketching.

If you cannot obtain these drawings from the builder or previous owner of the house, you'll have to make the site plan and floor plan yourself.

Topographic Survey

Unless you have a steeply sloping site and plan on modifying it considerably, you need not worry about obtaining this drawing. Ideally, any landscape planning is best accomplished with a topographic survey showing at least the elevations of a few key points on the site (spot elevations), if not contours (lines connecting points of the same elevation). However, practically speaking, most amateur residential landscape design (and much professional design) can be accomplished utilizing only the "calibrated eyeball" and simple tools like a line level (a small level hung on a taut string line). Site drainage patterns, which are clearly indicated on a topographic survey, can be observed first-hand during a rain and sketched on a sheet of paper for future use.

If you decide you need a topographic survey, you'll have to have a surveyor or civil engineer prepare it.

Measuring Your Site—An Easy Method

To begin with, you'll find a 50- or 100-foot measuring tape indispensable for taking measurements of your house and other features on your site. Shorter tapes can be used, but not as efficiently.

The general approach of this method is to establish for each major yard two base lines at right angles to each other. The accompanying sketch illustrates how to establish base lines in a front yard.

Set the "0" end of your tape at a distinct point such as the outer edge of the driveway and stretch it as far as it will go across the yard (a 100-foot tape will cross most typical yards with room to spare), keeping it parallel to the house walls. Then starting at the "0" point, walk along the tape until you are in line with some object on either side of the tape. Standing at the tape looking toward the

object, note the mark on the tape at the point where an imaginary line from you to the object crosses the tape perpendicular to it. The "object" may be a tree, an edge of the house, the edge of a window, etc. Note these dimension readings on your site measurement sketch (see the drawing on page 7).

Next, stretch the tape in a direction perpendicular to the first base line beginning at a logical place such as a house wall or the street curb. Repeat the procedure already described.

This base-line method works well for the larger spaces (front and back yards) and, despite appearances, is accurate enough. In smaller spaces and in order to obtain certain critical dimensions, you may have to measure directly with the tape from point to point in the normal manner.

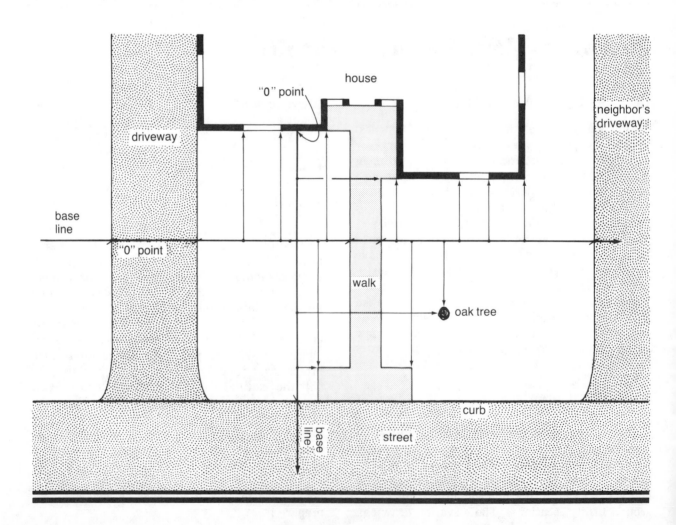

Drawing Materials You'll Need

The following materials will be useful in preparing the various plans discussed in this book. Although not all of them are totally necessary, you'll find the results better and in some cases easier to achieve if you use them.

Pencils

Use a #2 or #2½ medium-soft wooden pencil. #3 is too hard.

Pens

Broad-tipped felt markers in several colors. Fine-tipped felt pens.

Erasers

Standard types are sufficient. Artgum or kneaded rubber types are useful for erasing light lines or for cleaning drawings, but are not essential.

Paper

Professionals use tracing paper or sketch paper (transparent paper somewhat like onion skin typing paper) for preliminary sketches. It's available in rolls of varying length and width and is not very expensive. One roll should be all you'll need. You may be able to find something similar in large pads. Onion skin typing paper could be used for small sketches of portions of the plan.

For the base plan and the final plan, professionals use a semi-transparent paper available in rolls of varying lengths and widths. This paper is generally too expensive to be of use to the amateur, since it's only available in quantities much greater than you'll need. A better solution is to use a semi-transparent paper available in pads, either graph paper marked off at eight squares to the inch or plain drafting paper (not to be confused with sketch paper). Try to find paper large enough to draw your entire site on one sheet so that you don't have to tape together several smaller pieces.

A standard 8½ x 11 or 8½ x 14 ruled notepad will be useful for taking notes and making sketches during the program and site analysis stages.

Drawing Board

Optional. Several small sizes of inexpensive drawing boards are available. If you have a smooth-topped table of a comfortable height for drawing, use it.

Other Materials

Clip board (handy during roving note-taking sessions)

Standard ruler or architect's scale

Drafting tape (masking tape is too sticky and cellophane tape is difficult to remove after it's stuck down—both certainly can be used, however)

Straight edge (a draftsman's T-square, long ruler, stout yardstick, or other rigid and straight implement—it need not have markings)

Triangle (one, medium-sized, 45 degree or 30/60 degree. Used with a straight edge in order to make right angles)

Compass

Protractor

The Base Plan–What to Include

- Property lines, easements, building setback line

- House, garage and other existing structures such as tool shed, gazebo, greenhouse, fences, shade structures

- Driveway, walkways and paths, terrace, street curb

- Street lights, gas lights, mailbox, air conditioner, telephone company pedestal, ground-mounted electrical transformer, electrical panel boxes and meter on house or garage wall, gas meter, water meter, power poles, water faucets, barbecue grill (permanent), permanently-mounted play equipment (swing, fort, etc.)

- Utility lines (if the locations are known): water, underground or overhead electrical, gas, sanitary sewer, telephone, storm sewer (usually from enclosed courtyards, downspouts), septic tanks and drainfield

- Trees (individual trunk locations), shrubs (locate individually if large or separate, otherwise show mass outline), existing plant beds if you intend to keep them—if not, just list on a separate sheet of paper the plants you want to keep

- What to show on the house plan: windows, doors, electrical panel boxes and meter attached to out-side wall, water faucets attached to outside wall, point of entry of water into house, outdoor electrical outlets, exterior wall-mounted lights, exterior gas outlets, roof overhang, downspouts, sewer cleanouts in exterior walls (these need access), fireplace cleanout (needs access)

Don't label all of these items on the base plan; simply use a symbol. You can add labels later at the preliminary and final plan stages. Too much writing on the base plan can be confusing when you are trying to develop design ideas.

Useful Graphic Symbols

These are symbols for use on plan drawings. The ones that can be made quickly are best for preliminary sketching.

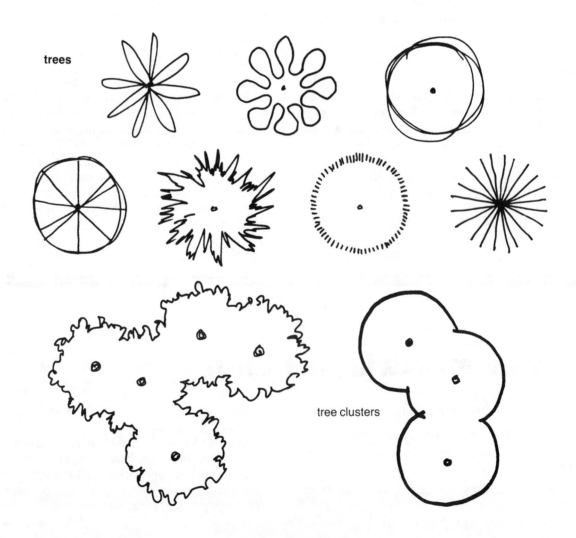

trees

tree clusters

shrubs

rows or hedges

grass

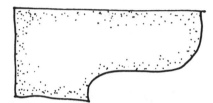

if you use this for grass,
don't use the similar indication for gravel

perennials

groundcovers

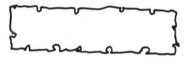 or

gravel

water

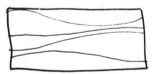

**brick or
tile pavement**

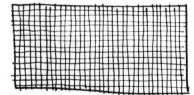

**fences and
walls**

Sun Angles in the South

The angle that the sun's path in the sky makes with the horizon is much the same throughout the South, as shown by these diagrams for two major southern cities. You can use the diagrams to determine approximately what the sun's noontime position would be at any given time of year. Knowing this and the directions east and west from your lot, you can determine approximately which areas of your yard will be in sun or shade at various times of day.

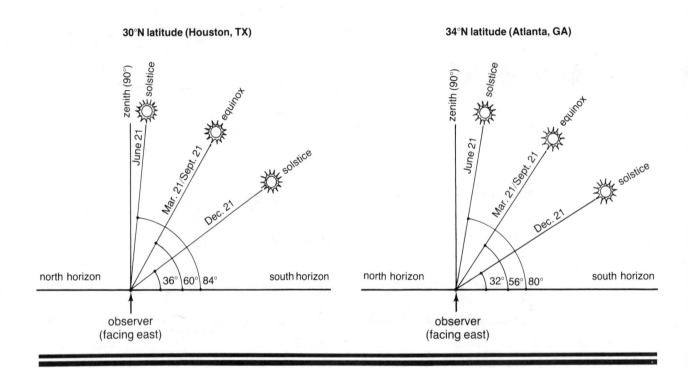

People—The Measuring Stick for Design

Landscape design, or any design for that matter, is for *people* in one way or another. In the home landscape, people are of paramount importance because they are in close contact with outdoor spaces and with the items in those spaces. Houses and furniture are designed with "people dimensions" in mind and landscapes should be too.

Surfacing

Walkway Widths

2'—minimum for garden path
3'—a one person walk
4'—accommodates two people uncomfortably
5'—accommodates two people comfortably

Step Dimensions

6″ riser/14″ tread (12″ is acceptable)
5″ riser/16″ tread
4″ riser/18″ tread
3″ riser/20″ tread

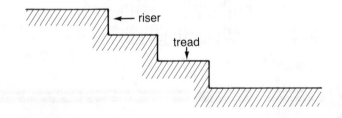

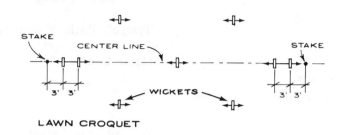

LAWN CROQUET

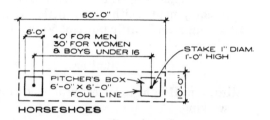

HORSESHOES

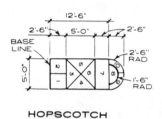

HOPSCOTCH

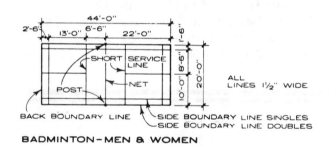

BADMINTON-MEN & WOMEN

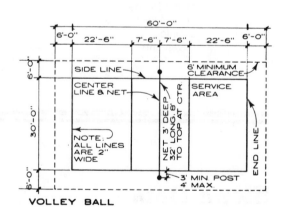

VOLLEY BALL

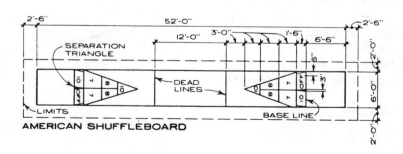

AMERICAN SHUFFLEBOARD

Stepping Stone Spacing: Totally dependent on the length of your stride. Measure it at the speed you'll be walking the path and space accordingly.

Driveways

Minimum width (one car): 9′
Desirable width (one car): 12′ (allows paved surface to step out on)
Minimum width (two cars): 16′
Desirable width (two cars): 20′ (allows paved surface to step out on)
Inside dimension of curves: approximately 15′-18′ radius but depends on the make of the car.
Parking stalls: 9′ x 18′ minimum

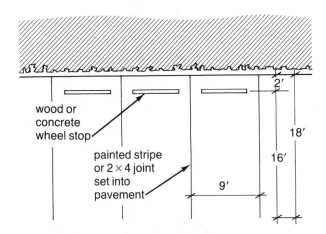

wood or concrete wheel stop

painted stripe or 2 × 4 joint set into pavement

2′
18′
16′
9′

Terrace Dimensions

Minimum to accommodate four chairs and a 3′ diameter table plus walking room: 10′ x 10′

Tricycle Path: 3′ minimum width

Game Courts

Enclosure

Average Eye-Level: 5′-5½′ above the ground
View-Screening Enclosure: 6′ minimum height on flat ground
Gates: 2′-6″ minimum width, 3′ preferable. If garden equipment must pass through, size according to equipment width plus a little extra.
Blocking Foot Traffic but Not View: 4′-5′ height

Shelter

Minimum Height to lowest protrusion for upright walking: 7′
Desirable Height: 7½′-8′ (average house ceilings are 8′)
Height of Structures attached to house is often governed by distance from ground to eaves of house (approximately 8′)

Average Height of Chairs or Benches: 16″-18″
Typical Residential Swimming Pool: 20′ x 40′, but size varies considerably, usually toward smaller dimensions.

Slope Data

An easy method for determining % of slope:
1. Place a carpenter's level on a 5-foot-long board and hold the board level with one end resting on the ground.
2. Measure the distance from the bottom of the free end of the board to the ground in feet and tenths of a foot.
3. Multiply the measurement by 20 = % of slope.

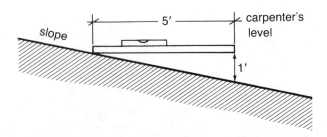

slope
5′
carpenter's level
1′

Example: 1′ x 20 = 20% or a 5 to 1 slope

% slope	slope ratio	slope angle
100%	1:1	45°
50%	2:1	26°
33⅓%	3:1	17°
25%	4:1	13°
20%	5:1	11°
10%	10:1	6°
5%	20:1	3°
1%	100:1	1°

Slope comparison diagram.

Minimum slopes for drainage

Material	Desirable	Marginal
Concrete (smooth finish)	1%	½%
Concrete (rough finish)	1½%	¾%
Brick and Tile	1½-2%	1%
Flagstone	1½-2%	1%
Fieldstone	2-3%	1½%
Asphalt	2%	1%
Compacted Material (iron ore)	2%	1%
Lawn Grass	2-3%	1%

Maximum slopes for various uses

Type of Use	Maximum Slope
Walks	5%
Ramps (pedestrian)	20%
Ramps (wheel chair)	8%
Ramps (automobiles)	12%
Terrace/Patio	3%
Lawn (maximum mowable)	33%
Lawn games	5%
Planting	50%
Cut Slope	100%
Fill Slope	50%

To determine the actual square footage of a sloped area shown in plan, multiply the square footage measured from the plan by the appropriate factor.

% of Slope	Horizontal Measure		Vertical Measure	Multiplying Factor
100%	1	to	1	1.4142
67%	1½	to	1	1.2019
50%	2	to	1	1.1180
40%	2½	to	1	1.0770
33%	3	to	1	1.0541
25%	4	to	1	1.0308
20%	5	to	1	1.0198

Landscape Surfacing– What Are the Choices?

Concrete
  Surface finishes: smooth troweled, wood float, broomed, exposed aggregate, salted, stamped. There are also several color options (paints and stains).
  Joint materials: boards and timbers of various sizes, brick, asphalt impregnated fiber board.

Asphalt: Cold mix (from sacks) or hot mix (from asphalt batch plants).

Brick
  Many color choices but few size options in paving bricks.
  Several standard laying patterns: running bond, jack-on-jack, basketweave, herringbone.

Tile
  Several color, size, and hardness options.
  Shapes: brick, square, hexagonal, moroccan.

Stone
  Cut stone, flagstone, fieldstone or ledgestone. Several color options.

Pre-Cast Concrete and Masonry Paving Pads: Plain or exposed aggregate finishes; use different sizes to create interesting patterns.

Wood Decks: Redwood, Cedar, Cypress, pressure-treated Southern Yellow Pine.

Iron Ore: The quality varies considerably from batch to batch.

Decomposed Granite: Same problems as iron ore.

River Gravel: A variety of colors and sizes are available but with much local variation.

Crushed Rock: Usually limestone but sometimes other local materials; several screened sizes available.

Crushed Brick: Localized availability.

Sand: Sharp sand, bank or river sand.

Blast Furnace Slag: Very localized sources.

Wood Rounds or Blocks: Rounds are sections of trees; blocks are short pieces of railroad ties or other heavy timbers set on end in a bed of sand.

Bark: Pine, Redwood, Fir; all are available as nuggets of various sizes; some are available in shredded or ground form.

Wood Chips: From tree trimming companies.

Hulls: Peanut, Pecan, Buckwheat, etc.

Lawn Grass: See the plant charts.

Groundcovers: See the plant charts.

Structural Enclosures–What Are the Choices?

Fences

The woods typically used for fencing are Cedar, Redwood, Cypress, and pressure-treated Southern Yellow Pine.

Solid Board: Different board widths and different board top designs available.

Board-on-Board: Boards placed on alternating sides of the fence; boards can be set horizontally or vertically.

Wood Slat: Slats (narrow boards—usually 1″ x 2″) can be butted together or spaced slightly apart.

Basketweave: Thin boards woven in and out on alternate sides of fence posts; boards are usually set horizontally.

Louvered: Boards can be set horizontally or vertically.

Lattice: Crisscrossed boards; many possible patterns using thin lath or standard sized boards.

Solid Panels: Plywood, hardboard, asbestos (sometimes available in colors), tempered glass, acrylic (clear or smoked).

Wood Picket: Many picket top designs to choose from.

Rail: Rails made of boards, split logs, round logs, timbers; different numbers of rails and different rail spacings add to the design possibilities.

Chain Link: Different wire gauges are available with or without vinyl coating in several colors. Use wood posts for an interesting variation.

Welded Wire Mesh: Wood or metal posts can be used.

Wrought Iron: Many design possibilities, all expensive.

Walls

Brick: Many colors and several brick size options. Walls can be solid (several brick patterns to choose from) or pierced (bricks spaced so as to leave holes through the wall).

Masonry Block: Blocks available in many sizes, solid or with decorative see-through designs. Solid block walls can be painted or surfaced with plaster to improve appearance.

Stone: Dry stacked or mortar set; many stones to choose from.

Stucco: Plaster on metal lath attached to a wood fence.

Concrete: Poured in place using wooden forms. Several surface finishes are possible: board-form, hand-rubbed, bush-hammered, sand-blasted; many other things can also be done to the surface of vertical concrete.

Within each type of enclosure there are many design possibilities depending on the materials used and the manner in which they are put together—too many, in fact, to list here.

Structural Shelters—
What Are the Material Choices?

Supporting Structure

Wood: Redwood, Cedar, Cypress, pressure-treated Southern Yellow Pine

Galvanized pipe: functional but not as good-looking as wood

Roof

Wood: same as above
Fiberglass reinforced plastic: corrugated or flat; clear or translucent
Acrylic: commonly called Plexiglas, which is a trade name; clear or smoked
Plastic mesh shade cloth: usually green or black
Canvas: short-lived

Miscellaneous Data

Area Calculations

1. Area formulas:
   Area of circle = 3.1416 x radius squared
   Area of right triangle = A + B ÷ 2
   Area of rectangle = length x width

2. To calculate the square footage of oddly shaped areas, divide the area into more manageable shapes as shown by the dashed line in the

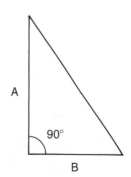

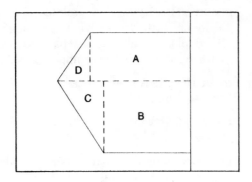
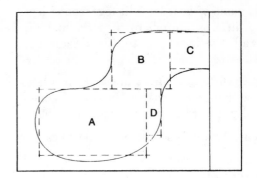

drawing. Do the same for irregular, free-form areas.

3. Groundcover multiplying factors: To determine the number of groundcover plants needed for a given area, multiply the area to be covered in square feet by the factor for the appropriate plant spacing.

Plant Spacing	Multiplying Factor
6″	4.0
8″	2.2
10″	1.5
12″	1.0
18″	.44
24″	.25
30″	.16
36″	.11
48″	.0625

Volume Calculations

1. 1 cubic yard = 27 cubic feet

To determine the quantity of topsoil, mulch, or gravel needed:
sq. ft. of area x depth of application (in ft.) ÷ 27 = cubic yards

Example: 154 sq. ft. x 4″ depth of topsoil (.33 ft.) = 50.82 cu. ft. ÷ 27 = 1.9 cu. yd.

Allow about 10% more for shrinkage.

Miscellaneous

1. Decimal equivalents (inches in decimals of a foot):

1″ = .08′	7″ = .58′
2″ = .17′	8″ = .67′
3″ = .25′	9″ = .75′
4″ = .33′	10″ = .83′
5″ = .42′	11″ = .92′
6″ = .50′	

2. Board Feet = length of board (in feet) x width of board (in inches) x thickness of board (in inches) ÷ 12

Cost Estimating – A Checklist of Items to be Included

Item	Unit of Measure
Grading	sq. ft. (cu. yd. if additional soil is required)
Drainage (pipe and inlet system)	linear ft. (pipe), Each (inlets)
Drainage (drain tile system)	linear ft. (pipe), cu. yd. (gravel)
Drainage (French drain system)	cu. yd. (gravel)
Utilities: water, sanitary sewer, natural gas electrical service	linear ft.
Sprinkler system (manual or automatic)	lump sum
Pavement (all types except stepping pads)	sq. ft.
Pavement (stepping pads)	Each
Pavement (loose and compacted materials)	cu. yd. or sq. ft.
Wood deck	sq. ft.
Fences	linear ft.
Walls (free standing)	linear ft. or sq. ft. of wall face
Retaining walls	sq. ft. of wall face or lump sum
Structural shelter	lump sum
Trellises and arbors	lump sum
Decorative pool and/or waterfall	lump sum
Swimming pool	lump sum
Greenhouse	lump sum
Garden lighting	lump sum
Outdoor furniture	Each
Trees	Each
Shrubs and vines	Each
Groundcover	Each
Grass	sq. yd.
Topsoil	cu. yd.
Mulch and soil conditioners (peat moss, bark, etc.)	cu. yd. (cu. ft. if in bags)
Erosion netting	sq. ft. or per roll
Edgers	linear ft.
Miscellaneous (fertilizer, root stimulator, herbicide, etc.)	

You should request pricing from contractors on the basis of the units listed.

Cost Estimate Worksheet

ITEM	SIZE	QUANTITY	UNIT PRICE	TOTAL PRICE

The Final Plan–What to Include

In addition to the items already shown on the base plan, your final plan should show everything you propose to install. If your landscape development includes very much construction, you may need to make two final plans, one for construction and one for planting. Too much information on one drawing clutters it and makes it difficult to read.

- Show critical dimensions of construction items (trellis, walkway, retaining wall, etc.) and their distance from some reference point such as a house wall or driveway edge. Include only enough dimensions to clearly locate the item and explain its size.

- Explanatory notes for the following should indicate specific materials, size at time of installation, quantity, and spacing (if appropriate):
    Edgers for plant beds
    Areas of loose surfacing material (sand, gravel, bark)
    All plants

- Label all items shown on the base plan and not previously labeled.

Southern Landscape Plants

The Plants Included in the Charts

The plants listed are the major ones used in the South, together with some lesser known but equally useful ones. Not all of the plants will grow in your climate. Among the list, however, can be found plants for all parts of the South, from the warmest sub-tropical areas of the lower South (zones 9 and 10) to the colder, more northern-like climates of the upper South (zone 7). Many of the plants whose southerly limit of easy culture is zone 7 are not listed simply for lack of space. Information about these can be found in books written for northern climates.

Unfortunately, lack of space prevents inclusion of the many perennials, annuals, bulbs, and tender tropical and sub-tropical plants that are also valuable additions to the southern landscape.

How to Use the Charts

Before attempting to use these plant charts, you should read the chapter on "Designing with Plants." There you will find an explanation of how the charts can best be used in the plant selection process.

All plants are listed alphabetically by their currently correct botanical names with their common names listed immediately below. To find a plant by its common name first, use the index following the charts.

The charts are most efficiently used in the following manner:

1. Place a plain 3 x 5 card on the chart with the longest edge of the card immediately below the column headings.

2. Mark on the card, for each column that is of importance to you, a dot or the appropriate letter or number depending on the graphic indication used in that column.

3. As you slide the card down the page, keeping the marks lined up with the appropriate columns, you can quickly find the plants that fit all or some of your requirements. A dot, letter, or number designation in a column means that the plant listed or one of its varieties has that characteristic or will grow in that situation. In the case of group listings (e.g., Pyracantha species and varieties), a column designation means that some plant within the group fulfills the requirements of the column. You'll have to research further in separate books to find the specific variety.

Explanation of Column Headings and Information

Many of the column headings in the charts are self-explanatory. A few, however, require a brief discussion.

Temperature Zones (7-10). These zones correspond to those on the Plant Hardiness Zone Map on page 101. Designations under these zonal headings indicate only whether the plant listed will or will not grow in that southern climatic zone, and do not necessarily indicate the plant's most northerly limit of cold hardiness in the United States.

Each zone includes within it many microclimatic areas not typical of the general zone characteristics (either colder or warmer). These zones, however, serve as good general indications of cold hardiness in the South.

An "F" in a zonal column means that the plant will freeze most, if not all, winters but will usually re-grow the following spring.

Soil/Moisture. A designation in these columns means that the plant listed will tolerate a fairly strong measure of the condition indicated.

Seashore Conditions. The numbers in this column indicate the seashore belt of exposure that the plant will tolerate.

Belt 1 conditions are the most severe. Plants listed for this belt will tolerate salt in the soil and in the air (salt spray), and constantly windy conditions with occasional wind-blown sand. These plants will withstand the full fury of a storm and most will endure contact with seawater.

Belt 2 conditions exist behind the protection of a natural or artificial barrier (fence, hedge of Belt 1 plants, etc.). Plants listed for this belt will tolerate salt in the soil and some in the air, but cannot withstand strong winds. Most of these plants cannot tolerate contact with seawater.

Belt 3 conditions are considerably milder than those of Belts 1 and 2. These plants will tolerate a little salt in the soil but none of the rigorous conditions of Belts 1 and 2. Small amounts of salt are still in the air in this belt but if regularly washed off the plants, no damage results. I have been conservative with this list. Probably, more plants will tolerate these conditions than are listed.

The information in this column is, for the most part, taken from Edwin Menninger's *Seaside Plants of the World: A Guide to Planning, Planting, and Maintaining Salt-Resistant Gardens*, Hearthside Press Inc., New York, 1964. Readers are referred to this book for an in-depth discussion of seashore gardening.

Growth Rate
F = Fast, M = Moderate, S = Slow

Foliage Texture
F = Fine, M = Medium, C = Coarse

Foliage Density
Op = Open, M = Moderately dense, D = Dense

Color
B = Blue
Br = Bronze
L = Lavender
Or = Orange

P = Purple
Pk = Pink
R = Red
V = Various colors available

Vi = Violet
W = White
Y = Yellow

Seasons
Sp = Spring
S = Summer
F = Fall
W = Winter
V = Various (blooms or produces fruit during several seasons)

ZONE 7   0° TO 10°
ZONE 8   10° TO 20°
ZONE 9   20° TO 30°

		TEMP				LIGHT		SOIL/MOISTURE					HEIGHT			SPREAD			SPECIAL FORMS								COLOR					USES		
Trees	Evergreen	Zone 7	Zone 8	Zone 9	Zone 10	Sun	Partial Shade	Acid	Alkaline	Dry	Wet	Seashore Conditions	20-35'	35-50'	Over 50'	Under 10'	10-30'	Over 30'	Weeping	Columnar	Pyramidal	Sculptural Branches	Growth Rate	Foliage Texture	Foliage Density	Decorative Bark	Fall Leaf Color	Flower Color	Flower Season	Fruit Color	Fruit Season	Espalier	Shade Tree	Pavement Breaker
Acer rubrum — Red Maple		•	•	•		•	•	•			•	3	•	•			•						M	C	D		R/Y	R	Sp	R	Sp		•	
Albizia julibrissin — Silk Tree (Mimosa)		•	•	•		•	•			•	•	2	•				•						F	F	Op			Pk	Su				•	
Betula nigra — River Birch		•	•	•	•	•	•	•			•		•				•						F	M	M	•	Y							
Butia capitata — Pindo Palm	•	•	•	•		•	•			•	•	3	•				•						S	C	Op					Or	Su			
Carya illinoinensis var's. — Pecan		•	•	•		•		•							•			•					F	M	D		Y						•	
Casuarina equisetifolia — Horsetail Tree	•		•	•	•	•	•	•	•	•	•	1	•	•				•			•		F	F	M/D									
Cedrus Deodara — Deodar Cedar	•	•	•	•		•	•			•		2		•				•			•		F	F	M									
Cercis canadensis — Eastern Redbud		•	•	•		•	•	•		•			•				•						M	C	D		Y	Pk	Sp					
Chionanthus virginicus — Fringe Tree		•	•	•		•	•	•					•				•						S	C	M		Y	W	Sp					
Cinnamomum Camphora — Camphor Tree	•		•	•		•	•					3		•				•					M	M	D								•	•
Cornus florida & var's. — Flowering Dogwood		•	•	•		•	•	•					•				•						S	C	Op		R	W/Pk	Sp	R	F			
Crataegus Phaenopyrum — Washington Hawthorn		•	•	•		•		•	•	•		3	•				•						M	M	M		R/Or	W	Sp	R	F			
Cupressus sempervirens 'Stricta' — Columnar Italian Cypress	•		•	•		•	•			•	•			•		•				•			M	F	D									
Eriobotrya japonica — Loquat	•		•	•	•	•	•	•	•	•	•	3	•				•						M/F	C	D			W	W	Y	Sp	•		
Eucalyptus cinerea — Silver Dollar Eucalyptus	•			•	•	•				•			•				•						F	M	Op	•								
Fraxinus velutina glabra — Modesto Ash			•	•	•	•				•	•				•			•					F	M	D		Y						•	•
Ginkgo biloba — Maidenhair Tree		•	•	•		•	•			•					•		•						S	F	M/D		Y						•	
Gleditsia triacanthos inermis var's. — Honey Locust		•	•	•		•				•	•	2			•			•					F	F	Op		Y							•
Ilex Cassine — Dahoon Holly	•	•	•	•		•	•	•			•	2	•				•						S	F	D					R	W			
Ilex opaca & var's. — American Holly	•	•	•	•		•	•	•				3	•				•						S	M	D					R	W			
Ilex vomitoria — Yaupon Holly	•	•	•	•		•	•	•		•	•	2	•				•					•	S	F	Op					R	W			
Koelreuteria bipinnata — Goldenrain Tree			•	•		•	•			•		2	•				•						F/M	M	D		Y	Y	Su/F	Or	F		•	
Lagerstroemia indica var's. — Crape Myrtle		•	•	•		•				•		3	•				•					•	S/M	F	Op	•	Y/R	V	Su					
Liquidambar styraciflua & var's. — Sweetgum		•	•	•		•	•	•			•				•			•			•		M	C	D		Y/R							
Liriodendron Tulipifera — Tulip Tree		•	•	•		•	•								•			•					F	C	D		Y							
Magnolia grandiflora & var's. — Southern Magnolia	•	•	•	•		•	•	•	•			3		•				•					S	C	D			W	Su	R	Su/F	•		•
Magnolia Soulangiana & var's. — Saucer Magnolia		•	•	•		•	•	•					•				•						S	C	D			W/Pk	Sp					
Malus species and varieties — Crabapple		•	•	•		•		•				2	•				•						M	M	M			W/Pk	Sp	R/Y	F	•		
Musa paradisiaca — Common Banana	•	F	F	•		•	•	•	•	•	•	3	•				•					•	F	C	Op									

Plant	Evergreen	Zone 7	Zone 8	Zone 9	Zone 10	Sun	Partial Shade	Acid	Alkaline	Dry	Wet	Seashore Conditions	20'-35'	35'-50'	Over 50'	Under 10'	10'-30'	Over 30'	Weeping	Columnar	Pyramidal	Sculptural Branches	Growth Rate	Foliage Texture	Foliage Density	Decorative Bark	Fall Leaf Color	Flower Color	Flower Season	Fruit Color	Fruit Season	Espalier	Shade Tree	Pavement Breaker
Olea europaea — Olive	•		•	•	•				•	•		2	•				•				•		S	F	D									
Parkinsonia aculeata — Retama			•	•	•	•			•	•		3	•				•						F	F	Op	•		Y	Sp Su				•	
Phoenix canariensis — Canary Island Date Palm	•		•	•	•	•			•	•		2		•			•						S	C	M					Or	F			
Pinus Elliottii — Slash Pine	•	•	•	•		•	•	•			•				•		•						M	F	Op									
Pinus halepensis — Aleppo Pine	•		•	•	•	•		•	•			1		•			•						.	F	D								•	
Pinus palustris — Longleaf Pine	•	•	•	•	•	•		•							•		•					•	S/M	F	Op									
Pinus Taeda — Loblolly Pine	•	•	•	•		•	•	•			•				•		•						M	F	Op									
Pinus Thunbergiana — Japanese Black Pine	•	•	•	•		•	•			•		3			•		•					•	S/M	F	Op									
Platanus occidentalis — American Planetree (Sycamore)		•	•	•	•	•				•		3			•			•					M	C	D	•							•	•
Podocarpus macrophyllus — Japanese Yew	•	•	•	•	•	•	•	•	•			2	•	•			•			•			S	F	D									
Prunus caroliniana — Cherry Laurel	•	•	•	•	•	•	•					3	•	•			•						M	M	D			W	W					
Prunus cerasifera 'Atropurpurea' — Purple Leaf Plum		•	•	•		•							•				•						F/M	M	D			W	Sp			•		
Pyrus Calleryana & var's. — Callery Pear		•	•	•		•			•				•				•						M	M	D		R	W	Sp					
Pyrus Kawakami — Evergreen Pear			•	•	•	•			•				•				•						M/M	C	D		V	W	W			•		
Quercus falcata & var's. — Southern Red Oak		•	•	•		•		•							•			•					M	C	D								•	•
Quercus nigra — Water Oak		•	•	•	•	•		•			•				•			•					M	M	D								•	•
Quercus phellos — Willow Oak		•	•	•		•		•			•				•			•					M	F	D		Y						•	•
Quercus Shumardii — Shumard Oak		•	•	•		•	•	•	•						•			•					M	C	D		R Y						•	•
Quercus virginiana — Live Oak	•	•	•	•	•	•		•	•			2		•				•					S/F	M	D								•	•
Sabal Blackburniana — Hispaniolan Palmetto	•		•	•	•		•					1	•				•			•			S	C	M									
Sabal Palmetto — Cabbage Palmetto	•		•	•	•		•					1	•				•			•			S	C	M									
Salix babylonica — Weeping Willow		•	•	•	•	•				•	•			•				•	•	•			F	F	D		Y							•
Sapium sebiferum — Chinese Tallow			•	•	•	•	•		•	•			•				•						F/F	M	M		R Or						•	•
Taxodium distichum — Bald Cypress		•	•	•	•	•		•			•	3			•		•				•		S	F	D		Br							
Trachycarpus Fortunei — Windmill Palm	•		•	•	•	•	•					2	•			•				•			S	C	M									
Ulmus crassifolia — Cedar Elm		•	•	•	•	•			•	•				•			•	•					S	F	D		Br						•	
Ulmus parvifolia & var's. — Chinese Elm (Evergreen Elm)		•	•	•		•			•			2					•	•					F/M	F	Op	•								
Washingtonia filifera — California Fan Palm	•		•	•	•	•			•	•		1		•			•			•			S	C	D									
Washingtonia robusta — Mexican Fan Palm	•	•		•	•	•			•	•		1			•		•			•			M	C	D									

Shrubs

*ALSO INCLUDES EVERGREEN SPECIES

Plant	Dec	Z7	Z8	Z9	Z10	Sun	Part Shade	Full Shade	Acid	Alk	Dry	Wet	Seashore	H<3'	H3-6'	H>6'	S<3'	S3-6'	S>6'	Weep/Arch	Round	Upright	Spread	Growth Rate	Foliage Texture	Fall Leaf Color	Flower Color	Flower Season	Fruit Color	Fruit Season	Variegated	Clipped Hedge	Tropical	Screening
Abelia grandiflora & var's. Glossy Abelia		•	•	•	•	•	•		•	•			2	•	•			•			•	•		•	M	F		W Pk	Su F					
Ardisia crenata Coralberry			•	•		•	•	•	•						•		•				•	•		S	M				R	F W				
Aucuba japonica & var's. Japanese Aucuba		•	•	•	•		•						1	•	•		•				•			M	C				R	W	•		•	
Bambusa glaucescens 'Fernleaf' Fernleaf Hedge Bamboo			•	•	•	•	•		•	•	•				•		•					•		F	F								•	•
Berberis Thunbergii 'Atropurpurea' Red Leaf Japanese Barberry	•	•	•	•	•	•	•		•				1		•		•				•			S	F	Y		Sp				•		
Brunfelsia pauciflora 'Floribunda' Yesterday-Today-and-Tomorrow			•	•			•	•	•						•		•				•			M	M		W Vi	Sp Su					
Buxus microphylla japonica Japanese Boxwood		•	•	•	•	•	•		•	•				•			•				•	•		S	F							•		
Callistemon citrinus Lemon Bottlebrush			•	•	•	•			•	•	•		2		•			•			•			F	F		R	Sp					•	•
Camellia japonica var's. Japanese Camellia		•	•	•			•		•						•	•	•				•	•		S	C		V	W Sp						
Camellia Sasanqua var's. Sasanqua Camellia			•	•			•		•						•	•	•				•			M	M		V	F W						
Carissa grandiflora var's. Natal Plum			•	•	•	•	•		•	•	•		1	•	•		•	•			•		•	M	M		W V	F	R	V		•		
Chaenomeles speciosa var's. Flowering Quince	•	•	•	•	•	•	•		•	•			2		•		•				•			M	M		V	W						
Chamaerops humilis Mediterranean Fan Palm			•	•	•	•	•		•	•			2		•		•				•			S	C								•	
Cleyera japonica Japanese Cleyera			•	•	•	•	•	•	•				3	•	•		•				•			M	F						•	•		
Cocculus laurifolius Snail Seed			•	•	•	•	•		•							•		•	•		•	•		M	C								•	
Cortaderia Selloana Pampas Grass		F	•	•	•	•			•	•	•	•	1		•		•	•			•	•		F	F		W Pk	Su F				•	•
Cotoneaster species and varieties Cotoneaster	*	•	•	•	•	•			•	•			2	•	•	•	•	•			•		•	M	M	R			R	W				
Cycas revoluta Sago Palm			•	•	•	•	•		•				3	•			•				•	•		S	C								•	
Elaeagnus pungens var's. Thorny Elaeagnus		•	•	•	•	•	•		•	•			1		•		•	•			•	•		F	M						•	•		•
Escallonia exoniensis 'Frades' Frades Escallonia			•	•	•				•				2		•		•				•			F	F		Pk	V				•		
Fatsia japonica Japanese Fatsia			•	•	•		•	•	•				3		•		•				•			F	C							•	•	
Feijoa Sellowiana Pineapple Guava			•	•	•	•			•	•	•		2		•		•				•			M	M		R	Sp Su						
Gardenia jasminoides & var's. Gardenia			•	•	•	•	•		•						•		•				•		•	M	F		W	Su F						
Hibiscus Rosa-sinensis var's. Chinese Hibiscus			F	•	•	•			•				3		•	•	•	•	•		•	•		F	C		V	Su			•		•
Hibiscus syriacus Shrub Althea	•	•	•	•	•	•	•		•	•			2		•		•				•			M	M		V	Su F						
Hydrangea macrophylla var's. Bigleaf Hydrangea	•	•	•	•	•		•	•	•				3		•		•				•			F	C		V	Su F			•		
Ilex cornuta var's. Chinese Holly		•	•	•	•	•	•		•	•	•		3	•	•	•	•	•			•			M	M				R	W		•		
Ilex crenata var's. Japanese Holly		•	•	•	•	•	•		•				2	•	•		•	•			•	•	•	S	F							•		
Ilex vomitoria & var's. Yaupon Holly		•	•	•	•	•	•		•	•	•	•	2	•		•		•			•	•		S	F				R	W		•		

	TEMP					LIGHT			SOIL/MOISTURE					HEIGHT			SPREAD			FORM						COLOR						USES		
Plant	Deciduous	Zone 7	Zone 8	Zone 9	Zone 10	Sun	Partial Shade	Full Shade	Acid	Alkaline	Dry	Wet	Seashore Conditions	Under 3'	3'-6'	Over 6'	Under 3'	3'-6'	Over 6'	Weeping/Arching	Rounded	Upright	Spreading	Growth Rate	Foliage Texture	Fall Leaf Color	Flower Color	Flower Season	Fruit Color	Fruit Season	Variegated Forms	Clipped Hedge	Tropical Effects	Screening Hedge
Jasminum Mesnyi — Primrose Jasmine			•	•	•	•	•		•	•	•		•		•			•		•	•	•		F	F		W Y	Sp						•
Juniperus species and varieties — Juniper		•	•	•	•	•	•			•	•		1 2	•	•	•		•	•	•	•	•	•	S M	F				•					
Justicia Brandegeana (Beloperone) — Shrimp Plant		F	F	•	•	•		•	•				•		•		•			•				F	M		Br Y	Sp Su						
Lagerstroemia indica dwarf var's. — Dwarf Crape Myrtle	•	•	•	•	•	•			•	•			3		•	•		•			•			S M	F	R Y	V	Su						
Leucothoe spp. — Leucothoe		•	•	•			•	•	•			•			•	•		•			•			S F / M M			W	Sp			•			
Ligustrum japonicum — Wax Leaf Ligustrum		•	•	•	•	•	•		•	•					•			•			•			M	M		W	Su			•	•		•
Ligustrum sinese 'Variegatum' — Variegated Chinese Privet		•	•	•	•	•	•		•	•					•			•			•			F	F		W	Su			•	•		•
Magnolia stellata & var's. — Star Magnolia	•	•	•	•		•	•		•				3		•			•			•			S	M		W Pk	Sp						
Mahonia Bealei — Leatherleaf Mahonia		•	•	•	•	•	•		•		•				•			•				•		S	C		Y	Sp	B	Su			•	
Michelia Figo — Banana Shrub		•	•	•	•	•	•		•				3		•			•				•		S	M		Y	Sp						
Nandina domestica & var's. — Common Nandina		•	•	•	•	•	•		•	•	•			•	•		•	•			•	•		S	F	R	W	Su	R	W				
Nerium Oleander var's. — Oleander		F	•	•	•	•			•	•	•		2		•	•	•	•			•			M / F	F		V	Sp Su					•	•
Osmanthus fragrans — Sweet Olive		•	•	•	•	•	•		•				3		•			•				•		S	M									
Philodendron Selloum — Selloum Philodendron			F	•	•	•	•	•	•				2		•	•	•	•						F	C								•	
Photinia Fraseri — Fraser's Photinia		•	•	•	•	•	•		•						•			•				•		F	M							•		•
Pittosporum Tobira & var's. — Green Pittosporum			•	•	•	•	•	•	•	•			1		•		•	•				•		M	F		W	Sp			•	•		•
Plumbago auriculata & var's. — Cape Plumbago			F	•	•	•			•				3		•	•	•	•		•			•	M	F		B W	V						
Podocarpus macrophyllus Maki — Shrubby Japanese Yew		•	•	•	•	•	•	•	•				2		•	•		•				•		S	F							•		
Pyracantha species and varieties — Pyracantha		•	•	•	•	•	•		•	•	•		3		•	•		•	•			•		F / M	F		W	Sp	Or	W				
Raphiolepis indica var's. — Indian Hawthorn		•	•	•	•	•			•	•			2		•			•				•		S	M		Pk W	Sp						
Rhododendron species and varieties — Azalea		•	•	•	•	•	•		•				3	•	•		•	•	•		•			S	F		V	Sp Su						
Spiraea Vanhouttei — Bridal Wreath	•	•	•	•	•	•	•		•	•					•			•		•	•			M	F		W	Sp						
Viburnum japonicum — Japanese Viburnum		•	•	•	•	•	•		•	•			2		•			•				•		M	C		W	Sp				•	•	•
Viburnum odoratissimum — Sweet Viburnum		•	•	•	•	•	•		•	•			2		•			•					•	S / M	C								•	•
Viburnum suspensum — Sandankwa Viburnum		•	•	•	•	•	•	•	•	•			2		•	•		•	•			•		S / M	C		W	W				•		•
Viburnum Tinus & var's. — Laurustinus Viburnum		•	•	•	•	•	•		•	•			3		•	•		•	•			•	•	S / M	M		W W		B	Su	•	•		•
Xylosma congestum — Shiny Xylosma			•	•	•	•	•		•						•			•				•		F	F							•		•
Yucca aloifolia — Spanish Bayonet			•	•	•	•			•		•		1		•			•					•	S	C		W	Su						
Yucca recurvifolia — Curved Leaf Yucca			•	•	•	•			•		•				•	•		•	•			•		S	C		W	Su					•	

Groundcovers

NOTE: ALL ARE EVERGREEN EXCEPT AS NOTED.

Plant	Zone 7	Zone 8	Zone 9	Zone 10	Sun	Partial Shade	Full Shade	Acid	Alkaline	Sand (S) or Clay (C)	Poor	Dry (D) or Wet (W)	Seashore Conditions	Under 6"	6"-1'	1'-1½'	Over 1½'	Under 2'	2'-5'	Over 5'	Grass-Like	Trailing/Running	Spreading Shrub	Mounding	Growth Rate	Foliage Texture	Flower Color	Flower Season	Fruit Color	Fruit Season	Variegated Forms	Stepping Stones	Steep Slopes	Cascading
Abelia grandiflora 'Prostrata' Prostrate Glossy Abelia*	•	•	•	•	•	•		•	•	S			2			•			•				•	•	F	F	W	S/F						•
Ajuga reptans & var's. Ajuga	•	•	•			•	•	•	•	C					•			•				R				F	F/M	B	Sp/Su			•	•	
Arctostaphylos Uva-ursi Bearberry	•	•	•	•	•	•		•		S	•	D	1	•					•				T			M/F	W	Sp	R	Su			•	•
Armeria maritima Sea Pink	•	•			•	•		•	•	S			1	•				•								M/F	Pk	Sp						
Arundinaria pygmaea Dwarf Bamboo*	•	•	•	•	•			•	•	•		D			•			•				R				F/M					•		•	
Asparagus densiflorus 'Sprengeri' Sprenger Asparagus	F	F	•	•	•	•		•	•	•		D	2		•		•							•	F	F			R	W				•
Carissa grandiflora var's. Natal Plum		•	•	•	•	•		•	•	•		D	1		•	•			•					•	M	M	W/V		R	V				•
Cotoneaster species and varieties Cotoneaster**	•	•	•		•			•	•	•		D	2	•	•	•	•						•	•	M/F	F/M			R	W			•	•
Cyrtomium falcatum Holly Fern		•	•		•	•	•	•		•			3		•		•							•	M	C								
Dichondra micrantha Dichondra		•	•	•		•	•	•		•			3	•		•			•			R				F	F						•		
Duchesnea indica Mock Strawberry	•	•	•	•	•	•		•	•	•					•	•			•			R				F	F	Y/V		R	V		•		•
Euonymus Fortunei & var's. Wintercreeper	•	•	•	•	•	•	•	•	•	•			1	•	•	•			•			T		•	M	M/F					•		•	•
Festuca ovina glauca Blue Fescue	•	•	•	•	•	•		•	•	S	•	D	2	•		•			•	•					F	F								
Fragaria var's. Strawberry	•	•	•	•	•	•		•		•				•			•					R				F	C	W/V		R	V				
Gardenia jasminoides 'Radicans' Dwarf Gardenia		•	•	•	•	•		•							•	•			•				•	•	M	F	W	Su						
Gelsemium sempervirens Carolina Jessamine	•	•	•	•	•	•		•		•			3		•		•				•	T		•	F	F	Y	Sp						•
Glechoma hederacea Ground Ivy	•	•	•	•	•	•	•	•	•	•			3	•		•			•			R				F	M	B	Sp/Su			•	•	
Hedera canariensis Algerian Ivy		•	•	•	•	•	•	•	•	•			1		•				•			T				F	C					•		•	•
Hedera Helix & var's. English Ivy	•	•	•		•	•	•	•	•	•			2		•				•			T				M/F	C					•		•	•
Heuchera sanguinea & var's. Coral Bells	•	•	•		•	•			•	S			2	•		•							•		M	M	V	Sp/Su						
Hypericum calycinum Dwarf Hypericum	•	•	•	•	•	•		•	•	•		D			•		•	•				R				F	M	Y	Su					•	
Ilex cornuta 'Rotunda' Dwarf Chinese Holly	•	•	•		•	•		•	•	•		D	3		•	•			•					•		S	M								
Ilex crenata 'Helleri' Dwarf Japanese Holly	•	•	•		•	•		•	•	•			2		•				•					•		S	F								
Ilex vomitoria 'Nana' Dwarf Yaupon	•	•	•		•	•		•	•	•		•	2		•				•					•		S	F								
Juniperus chinensis procumbens Japanese Garden Juniper	•	•	•	•	•	•		•	•	•		D	2		•		•			•			•	•	S	F							•	•
Juniperus chinensis Sargentii Sargent Juniper	•	•	•	•	•	•		•	•	•		D	2		•				•	•			•	•	S	F							•	•
Juniperus conferta 'Blue Pacific' Blue Pacific Shore Juniper	•	•	•	•	•	•		•	•	•		D	1	•				•				T			S	F							•	•
Juniperus horizontalis var's. Prostrate Juniper	•	•	•	•	•	•		•	•	•		D	2	•	•	•			•			T			S	M/F							•	•
Juniperus Sabina var's. Savin Juniper	•	•	•	•	•	•		•	•	•		D	2		•	•			•				•	•	S	F							•	•

*Semi-Evergreen **Some Evergreen. Some Deciduous

Groundcovers

Plant	Zone 7	Zone 8	Zone 9	Zone 10	Sun	Partial Shade	Full Shade	Acid	Alkaline	Sand (S) or Clay (C)	Poor	Dry (D) or Wet (W)	Seashore Conditions	Under 6"	6"-1'	1'-1½'	Over 1½'	Under 2'	2'-5'	Over 5'	Grass-Like	Trailing/Running	Spreading Shrub	Mounding	Growth Rate	Foliage Texture	Flower Color	Flower Season	Fruit Color	Fruit Season	Variegated Forms	Stepping Stones	Steep Slopes	Cascading
Liriope Muscari & var's. Liriope	•	•	•	•	•	•	•	•	•	•			3		•		•				•				S	F	P	Su			•			
Liriope spicata Creeping Liriope	•	•	•	•	•	•		•	•	•			2		•		•				•				M	F	L	Su						
Lonicera japonica chinensis Purple Japanese Honeysuckle	•	•	•	•	•	•		•	•	•	•	•	2				•					T		•	F	M	W Sp / P	Su					•	•
Lonicera japonica 'Halliana' Hall's Honeysuckle	•	•	•	•	•	•		•	•	•	•	•	2				•					T		•	F	M	W Sp / Y	Su					•	•
Lysimachia Nummularia Moneywort	•	•	•		•	•		•	•	C		W		•					•			R			F	F						•	•	
Ophiopogon japonicus Monkey Grass	•	•	•	•	•	•	•					W	2		•		•				•			•	S	F								
Pachysandra terminalis Japanese Pachysandra	•	•	•			•	•	•		•			2		•				•			R		•	M	M					•		•	
Paxistima Canbyi Canby Paxistima	•	•	•		•	•		•								•			•			T		•	S	F								
Phlox subulata & var's. Moss Pink	•	•	•		•			•	•	•	•					•			•			T			F	F	Pk W	Sp						•
Pittosporum Tobira 'Wheelers Dwarf' Wheeler's Dwarf Pittosporum		•	•	•	•	•		•		•			1				•		•					•	S / M	F								
Potentilla Tabernaemontani Spring Cinquefoil	•	•	•	•	•	•		•	•	•					•							R			F	F	Y	V			•	•		
Pyracantha species and varieties Pyracantha	•	•	•	•	•							D	3			•			•					•	F / M	F	W	Sp	R F / Or	W				
Rosmarinus officinalis 'Prostratus' Dwarf Rosemary		•	•	•	•			•	•	•	•	D	1		•	•						T		•	M / F	F	W / B	Sp						•
Santolina Chamaecyparissus Gray Santolina	•	•	•	•	•			•	•	•	•	D	1		•	•								•	S / M	F	Y	Su					•	•
Santolina virens Green Santolina	•	•	•	•	•			•	•	•	•	D	1		•									•	F	F	Y	Su					•	•
Saxifraga stolonifera Strawberry Begonia	•	•	•	•		•	•	•	•					•				•				R			M / F	C	Sp / W	Su			•			
Sedum lineare Stringy Stonecrop	•	•	•	•	•	•		•	•	•	•	D	2	•			•					T			F	F	Y	Sp						•
Sedum rupestre Sedum rupestre	•	•	•	•	•			•	•	•	•	D	2	•	•		•					T			F	F	Y	Su						•
Sedum spurium & var's. Two Row Stonecrop*	•	•	•	•	•			•	•	•	•	D	2	•			•					T			F	M	Pk R	Su						•
Senecio Cineraria Dusty Miller	•	•	•	•	•					S		D	1		•		•							•	F	C	Y	Su						•
Thymus Serphyllum Mother-of-Thyme	•	•	•	•	•			•	•	S		D	2	•			•					T			F	F	L	Su				•		•
Trachelospermum jasminoides Confederate Jasmine		•	•	•	•	•		•	•	•			1			•		•				T		•	F	M	W	Sp			•			•
Trachelospermum jasminoides pubescens Dwarf Confederate Jasmine		•	•	•	•	•		•	•	•			1		•		•					T		•	M	F					•			
Verbena peruviana Peruvian Verbena		•	•	•	•			•	•	•		D		•			•					T			F	F	R	V			•		•
Vinca major Bigleaf Periwinkle	•	•	•	•	•	•		•	•	•			3			•		•				T			M / F	M	L Sp / B	Su			•		•	•
Vinca major Dwarf Periwinkle	•	•					•									•						T		•	M	F	B Sp	F						•
Viola odorata Sweet Violet	•	•	•	•		•	•	•	•	•					•		•							•	F	M	Vi	Sp						
Wedelia trilobata Wedelia		F	•	•	•			•	•	•		W	2			•	•		•			T		•	F	M	Y	V						•
Zoysia tenuifolia Korean Grass		•	•	•	•	•		•	•	•				•					•					•	S	F					•			

*Semi-Evergreen

Plant	Evergreen	Zone 7	Zone 8	Zone 9	Zone 10	Sun	Partial Shade	Full Shade	Acid	Alkaline	Dry	Wet	Seashore Conditions	High	Moderate	Low	Twining	Tendrils	Clinging	Needs Tying	Growth Rate	Foliage Texture	Foliage Density	Fall Leaf Color	Flower Color	Flower Season	Variegated Forms	Suitable as Shelter	Groundcover Also
Antigonon leptopus — Coral Vine			F	F	•	•	•			•	•	•	3	•		•					F	C	D		Pk	Su F			
Bignonia capreolata — Cross Vine	•	•	•	•	•	•	•		•			•		•		•					M	M	M		Y Or	Sp		•	
Bougainvillea species and var's. — Bougainvillea	•			F	•	•							2	•						•	F	M	D		V	Su	•		•
Campsis radicans — Trumpet Vine		•	•	•	•	•	•						2	•					•		F	F	D		Or	Su F			
Campsis Tagliabuana 'Mme.Galen' — Mme. Galen Trumpet Vine		•	•	•	•	•	•						2	•					•		F	F	D		R Or	Su F			
Clematis dioscoreifolia — Sweet Autumn Clematis	•	•	•	•	•	•	•			•			2		•						F	M	D		W	Su F			
Clematis var's. (large flowered) — Clematis		•	•	•		•	•			•						•	•	•			F	M	M		V	V			
Clytostoma callistegioides — Lavender Trumpet Vine	•		F	•	•	•	•	•					3			•					M F	M	D		L	Sp			
Dioscorea bulbifera — Air Potato		F	F	F	•	•						•	2				•				F	C	D						
Fatshedera Lizei — Fatshedera	•		•	•	•	•	•		•											•	M C		Op				•		
Ficus pumila — Climbing Fig Vine	•		•	•	•	•	•		•	•			3	•					•		M F	M	D				•		
Gelsemium sempervirens — Carolina Jessamine	•	•	•	•	•	•	•		•			•	3	•							F	F	M Op		Y	Sp		•	•
Hedera canariensis — Algerian Ivy	•		•	•	•	•	•	•					1						•		F	C	D				•	•	•
Hedera Helix & var's. — English Ivy	•	•	•	•	•		•	•					2	•					•		F	C	D				•	•	•
Lonicera japonica chinensis — Purple Japanese Honeysuckle	•	•	•	•	•	•	•		•	•	•	•	2	•		•					F	M	D		W P	Sp Su		•	•
Lonicera japonica 'Halliana' — Hall's Honeysuckle	•	•	•	•	•	•	•		•	•	•	•	2	•		•					F	M	D		W Y	Sp Su		•	•
Lonicera sempervirens — Trumpet Honeysuckle	•	•	•	•	•	•	•								•	•					M	M	M Op		R	Su			
Macfadyena Unguis-cati (Doxantha) — Cat's Claw	•		F	•	•	•	•			•						•			•		F	M	D M		Y	Sp		•	
Parthenocissus quinquefolia — Virginia Creeper		•	•	•	•	•	•	•	•	•			1	•					•		F	C	D	R				•	
Parthenocissus tricuspidata — Boston Ivy		•	•	•	•	•	•	•	•	•			1	•					•		F	C	D	R				•	
Passiflora alatocaerulea — Passion Vine	•			•	•	•	•						3			•					F	M	D		W	Su			
Rosa Banksiae var's. — Lady Banks' Rose	•	•	•	•	•	•			•	•			2							•	F	F	M		W Y	Sp			
Rosa (climbing varieties) — Rose		•	•	•	•				•	•			3		•					•	M	M	F Op		V	V			
Trachelospermum jasminoides — Confederate Jasmine	•		•	•	•	•	•		•	•			1	•		•			•		F	M	D		W	Sp	•	•	•
Vitis species and varieties — Grape		•	•	•	•	•	•		•	•					•	•					F	C	D					•	
Wisteria floribunda — Japanese Wisteria		•	•	•	•	•	•		•	•					•	•					F	F	M		Vi	Sp			
Wisteria sinensis — Chinese Wisteria		•	•	•	•	•	•		•	•					•	•					F	F	M		Vi	Sp			

Column groups: **TEMP** (Evergreen, Zone 7–10) · **LIGHT** (Sun, Partial Shade, Full Shade) · **SOIL/MOISTURE** (Acid, Alkaline, Dry, Wet, Seashore Conditions) · **HEIGHT** (High, Moderate, Low) · **GROWTH HABIT** (Twining, Tendrils, Clinging, Needs Tying, Growth Rate, Foliage Texture, Foliage Density) · **COLOR** (Fall Leaf Color, Flower Color, Flower Season, Variegated Forms) · **USES** (Suitable as Shelter, Groundcover Also)

Lawns	Below 10°F	Partial Shade	Acid	Alkaline	Sandy	Clay	Dry	Wet	Seashore Conditions	Slow	Fast	Fine	Medium	Coarse	Open	Moderate	Dense	½"	1"	1"-2"	2"	Seed	Sprigs or Sod	High Maintenance	Low Maintenance
Bermuda Grass *Cynodon Dactylon*																									
Common			●	●	●	●	●		2	●	●				●	●				●		●	●	●	
Ormond			●	●	●	●	●		2	●	●					●			●				●	●	
Tifdwarf			●	●	●	●	●		2	●	●						●	●					●	●	
Tifgreen		●	●	●	●	●	●		2	●	●						●	●	●				●	●	
Tiflawn			●	●	●	●	●		2	●	●					●				●			●	●	
Tifway			●	●	●	●	●		2	●	●					●			●				●	●	
Centipede Grass *Eremochloa ophiuroides*																									
Common		●	●			●					●		●			●				●		●	●		●
Oaklawn		●	●			●	●				●		●			●				●		●			●
St. Augustine Grass *Stenotaphrum secundatum*																									
Common		●		●	●	●		●	2	●				●		●				●			●	●	
Bitter Blue		●		●	●	●		●	2	●				●		●				●			●	●	
Floratam				●	●	●		●	2	●				●	●						●		●	●	
Floratine		●		●	●	●		●	2	●			●	●	●					●			●	●	
Zoysia Grass *Zoysia species and varieties*																									
Emerald (Z. 'Emerald')	●	●	●	●	●	●	●		3	●		●				●				●			●	●	●
Manila Grass (Z. Matrella)	●	●		●	●	●	●		3	●			●			●				●	●	●	●	●	
Meyer (Z. japonica 'Meyer')	●	●	●	●	●	●	●		3	●			●			●				●		●		●	
Carpet Grass **Axonopus affinis**		●	●		●			●			●			●		●				●	●	●	●		●

Index